"Having read Arthur Bennett's *The Valley of Vision* multiple times, I've always hoped someone else would mine the writings of the Puritans for more Scripture-drenched, Christ-exalting, God-glorifying, heartfelt prayers. My wait is over. Tim Chester has produced a volume eminently useful for private devotions, public gatherings and personal reflection. I expect his carefully chosen, thoughtfully organized, and beautifully edited prayers will serve the church for many generations to come."

BOB KAUFLIN
Director, Sovereign Grace Music

"These superb prayers model and teach a rich, deep devotion to God—Father, Son and Holy Spirit. Soaked in Scripture, they are wonderfully realistic about the life of faith. From a prayer for unbelieving children to a prayer with a dying Christian, with every style from the gripping logic of John Owen to the passionate warmth of Samuel Rutherford, these old believers walk with us in deepening our own lives of prayer. Tim Chester has done us a great service in editing and updating them so beautifully and clearly."

CHRISTOPHER ASH
Writer in Residence, Tyndale House

"I greatly appreciate the effort Tim Chester has gone to in this beautiful book, not only to organise and translate the biblically and doctrinally rich words of the Puritans into a language I can pray myself today, but also to note where these exquisite treasures can be found in their original settings. Full of arresting images and comforting truths, this is a precious resource to come back to time and again for spiritual refreshment, pastoral challenge, and pure adoration of our gracious and sovereign God."

LEE GATISS
Series Editor, The Complete Works of John Owen

"These pages are a great gift from Dr Tim Chester to help us 'to glorify God, and to enjoy him for ever' and to experience the love of Christ, as Paul says, 'together with all the saints'. There is something in *Into His Presence* to help all of us to experience communion with God in every situation of life. Tim Chester has given us a treasure trove."

SINCLAIR B. FERGUSON
Chancellor's Professor of Systematic Theology, Reformed Theological Seminary

"The apostle Paul wrote that 'we do not know what to pray for as we should'. All Christians find themselves, from time to time, knowing they need to pray but not knowing how. These prayers, taken from the writings of our brothers and sisters of the past, are a blessed guide to prayer when we lack words of our own."

ERIC SCHUMACHER
Pastor, author and songwriter

"The Puritans knew their God, not just in their brains, but in the bruises of life's afflictions, and they sought him with all their hearts. Tim Chester brings us into the Puritans' prayer closet to learn from their devotion. Some of these selections are Puritan prayers, some are the thoughts and phrases of Puritan teachings freshly woven into prayers, and all are fervent pantings of the soul after the glorious, triune God."

JOEL R. BEEKE
President, Puritan Reformed Theological Seminary

TIM CHESTER

INTO HIS PRESENCE

Praying with the Puritans

thegood**book**
COMPANY

Into His Presence: Praying with the Puritans
© Tim Chester, 2022.

Published by:
The Good Book Company

thegoodbook

COMPANY

thegoodbook.com | thegoodbook.co.uk
thegoodbook.com.au | thegoodbook.co.nz | thegoodbook.co.in

ISBN: 9781784987770 | Printed in India

Design by Ben Woodcraft

CONTENTS

INTRODUCTION

Without often seeking God, the vitality of the soul is lost.
We may as well expect a harvest without sowing, as any
liveliness of grace where there is no seeking God.
                                                    —*Thomas Manton*[1]

The Puritans were people of prayer. Many Puritan pastors rose early to pray, like Joseph Alleine who spent the time between 4am and 8am in personal worship, and felt ashamed if he heard the blacksmith at work before he was at prayer. Each year Isaac Ambrose took himself off into the woods for a month to spend uninterrupted time alone in prayer and meditation. Puritan families were encouraged to read the Scriptures and pray together each morning and evening, with pastors providing model prayers for those who were unsure where to begin.

Yet the Puritans were not fixated on prayer itself; they were fixated on God. Prayer was merely the means; it was God himself who was their goal. Their spirituality was characterised by a big view of God. They felt keenly the vast gulf between God's holiness and human sinfulness—a gulf into which a Christian might have plunged were it not for God's grace to us in Christ. Again and again in their prayers we see a recognition of the depths of our sin enlarging a vision of the heights of Christ's love.

Their big vision of God did not mean their God was remote. Quite the opposite. His activity permeated the whole of life. The Puritans had a high view of God's providence. All their comforts came from his hand and were to be received with gratitude. But hardships, too, were part of his mysterious design. All of life—from daily prayers to work and home life—was to be lived before God, with his help.

~

I love doing cryptic crosswords. My aim is to start one at breakfast and finish it during my mid-morning tea break. See if you can work out this clue:

Strait-laced girl enters into the joke.

The answer is "puritan". "Girl enters into joke" is the cryptic part of the clue ("pu[rita]n"). The straight part of the clue is, if you'll excuse the pun, "strait-laced". It's an example of the bad press with which Puritanism has often been dogged. The implication is that the Puritans opposed fun.

It's true that Puritans were serious about their faith. But, as the prayers in this book reveal, they also enjoyed life. They expressed gratitude to God for food, fun and friendship. Even more, they enjoyed God. They pursued the pleasures of God.

Puritanism began in England in the second half of the 16th century, during the reign of Elizabeth I, as a reform movement within the Church of England. Its passion was to see a church shaped by the Bible with a gospel of justification by faith alone. Many of its early leaders had escaped the persecutions of Mary I in the 1550s through exile in Europe. Here they were strongly influenced by the Reformed tradition. Their hopes for spiritual renewal were dashed when James I, Elizabeth's successor, showed no interest in radical reform. This was when the Pilgrim Fathers set sail for safety in America. Then, under Charles I, Puritans were often persecuted.

The Commonwealth of Oliver Cromwell gave Puritans a voice in national affairs. But it was short-lived. The monarchy was restored in 1660, and in 1662 hundreds of Puritans were forced out of the Church of England in "the Great Ejection". Many went underground, holding secret meetings (called "conventicles") or gathering congregations in their homes. But by the end of the 17th century the movement had ceased to exist as a distinct force in national life.

Yet the spirituality of Puritanism lives on in its writings. Here we find a rich store of treasures which continue to provide both theological clarity and pastoral comfort. It is these treasures I have plundered in this book. Around half the prayers in this book are Puritan prayers which I've edited. The other half I've created out of descriptive passages from Puritan sermons or books. In both cases I've updated the language while trying to retain the feel of the original writers. Choosing extracts was not easy. Samuel Bolton, John Bunyan, Jeremiah Burroughs and Ezekiel Hopkins were all well represented on the shortlist, but somehow didn't quite make the final cut.

I hope that this book will give you a flavour of Puritan spirituality that might prompt you to explore their writing further. But that has not been my primary aim. My primary aim has been to provide prayers to be prayed. These prayers are not historical curiosities; they are powerful expressions of faith that can enrich our spiritual lives. That's why I've organised them under headings that flag up when and how they might be used. They're designed to be put to work. You could read one a day, but you can also turn to them in need. You could use them on your own, but you can also use them in public worship.

The Puritan Ezekiel Hopkins describes God as "the great proprietor". Everything we could desire—whether spiritual or temporal blessings, whether greater faith, love, patience or humility—are on the shelves in God's great department store (or in the catalogue of his online outlet). And prayer, says Hopkins, is "a means appointed by God to obtain those blessings and mercies of which we stand in need". Then he changes the imagery:

> *Our prayers and God's mercy are like two buckets in a well. While the one ascends, the other descends. So, while our prayers ascend to God in heaven, his mercies and blessings descend upon us.[2]*

Here are 80 prayers to fill our buckets with before we send them up to God, and wait for his bucket of blessing to come down to us.

PRAYERS OF PRAISE
TO THE FATHER

1. Kind and Tender

Loving Father, may we see you as love,
    not with anxious and doubtful thoughts,
    nor questioning your good-will and kindness,
        but seeing in your heart
            the fountain of all goodness.
May we not look on you as a frowning father,
      but as a Father who is most kind and tender.
For your love is the love of one who is all-sufficient,
    infinitely satiated with yourself
                and your glorious perfections,
      with no need to look for love in others.
There might you have rested in contentment for ever,
    rejoicing in your Son for all eternity,
      but you chose to love your saints,
      seeking not your satisfaction alone, but our good.
This is your love, the love of a Father,
      going out in kindness and bounty.

Your love is an eternal love,
    fixed on us before the foundation of the world,
    before we were, or had done, the least good.
This thought alone makes all that is within us leap for joy.
We prostrate our souls in humble, holy reverence,
    and rejoice before you with trembling.

Help us, we pray, to believe
    that such is your fatherly heart towards us.
May our minds know it,
    may our wills embrace it,
        may our affections be filled with it.
Let us be bound with the cords of this love.
This is your great pleasure, Father,
    that we see you
        full of love
            and tenderness
                and kindness towards us.
Flesh and blood are so apt to have hard thoughts of you.
We are afraid to think well of you.
We think it a boldness to look on you
    as good, gracious, tender, kind, loving.
Assure us, we pray,
    that there is nothing more acceptable to you
    than for us to keep our hearts close to you
        as the eternal fountain of all that rich grace
            which flows out to sinners in the blood of Jesus.
As we sit down a little at this fountain,
    may we discover the sweetness of its streams.
And so may we, who once ran from you in fear,
    not be able to keep at a distance—even for a moment.

JOHN OWEN

2. YOU ARE OUR GOD

O God, you are our God:
  our strong tower, our fountain of living water,
    our Father, a Father of mercies,
    an everlasting Father in heaven.

O God, you are our God,
  by your grace planted in us,
  and by the pledge of your Spirit.
May he stamp the imprint of holiness in our hearts;
        embroidering and bespangling our souls,
        making them glorious within.
May he, by his magnetic virtue, draw our hearts to you:
    our paradise of delight and our chief treasure!
May our hearts be so chained to you
  that nothing else can enchant us or draw us from you.
Though our flesh be on earth,
  may our hearts be in heaven.
When you say to our souls, "You are mine,"
  may our souls answer: "Lord, we are yours;
      all I have is at your service;
      my head shall be yours to study you;
      my tongue shall be yours to praise you."

O God, you are our God,
  and so, though we may feel the stroke of evil,

we do not feel the sting,
    for nothing can ultimately hurt us.
If we lose our name—it is written in the book of life.
If we lose our liberty—our conscience is free.
If we lose our belongings—
    we possess the pearl of great price.
If we meets with storms—
    we know where to put in for harbour.
When there is a storm outside,
    you can make music within.
Our souls are safe, as in a garrison,
    hid in the promises,
        hid in the wounds of Christ;
            hid in your eternal decree.

O God, you are our God, and all that is in you is ours.
You say to us: "All that I have shall be yours;
        my wisdom shall be yours to teach you;
        my power shall be yours to support you;
        my mercy shall be yours to save you."
We may lose everything else,
    but we cannot lose you:
you are ours *from* everlasting in election
    and *to* everlasting in glory.

Thomas Watson

3. One String to the Bow

Lord God, you and you alone
    should be the sole object of our trust.
May there be but one string to the bow of our faith:
    that is you, our Lord.
May we not rest in any thing other than you.
Forgive us when we trust in our heads,
    for our own understanding is an unsafe place to lean.
Forgive us when we trust in our hearts,
    for they are so deceitful and wicked.
Forgive us when we trust in our vigour,
    for our hands will soon hang down and faint.
Forgive us when we trust in any excellences,
    for the best of us in our best state is altogether vanity.
Forgive us when we trust in riches,
    for riches are fair-faced nothings,
    taking flight like birds.
Forgive us when we trust in human allies,
    for they prove not to be staffs but broken reeds.

But on this the arm of trust may safely lean:
    your almighty arm and power;
    and your infinite goodness, mercy, and bounty.

Thomas Lye

4. Resting on God's Attributes

Lord God, how I thank you
  because you have given me yourself,
  and an interest in all your glorious attributes:
  whatever is in you shall be mine, and for me.
Oh, what encouragement to faith:
      to be assured that all your attributes are mine;
      as much mine as the drink in my cup
          and the food on my plate.
May the hands of my faith take hold of these two handles:
          that you are willing and able.
For there is no condition into which I can fall
  but some divine attribute can support me.

I rest on your omnipotence
  when surrounded by troubles and dangers.
When I am called to difficult duties above my strength,
  strong lusts to oppose,
      violent temptations to resist,
          weighty employments to undertake,
          may faith support me on your omnipotence.

I rest on your omniscience
  when I don't know what to do,
  when I'm at my wit's end,
      for you know how to deliver the righteous.

When I'm afraid my treacherous heart will deceive me,
when I'm worn down by Satan's accusations,
    let your omniscience support me.

I rest on your immensity
    when deserted by friends, or separated from them,
    or when I fear remote intrigues in other countries,
for you, Lord, are everywhere.

I rest in your all-sufficiency.
    Do I want riches? You are all-sufficient.
    Do I want liberty? You are liberty.
    Do I want comfort? You are in the means of grace.
    Do I fear death? You are life.
    Do I fear being cast off? You are unchangeable.

I rest in your mercy.
There is no condition so low that mercy cannot reach it,
    none so bad that mercy cannot better it,
    none so bitter that mercy cannot sweeten it,
    none so hopeless that mercy cannot comfort in it.

I rest in your purity.
For in your jealousy of sin,
    you will be a consuming fire to my lusts, but not to me.
I rest in your justice.
Lord, I have sinned, and deserve your wrath;
    but Christ, my Surety, has done and suffered

all that your righteous law requires.
He was wounded for my transgressions,
    and your justice will not punish
        the same offences twice.

Riches are an uncertain, unsatisfying, limited,
    deceitful nothing.
You are an unchangeable, satisfying, all-sufficient,
    faithful everything.

I am full of sin;
    you are merciful.
I am unworthy;
    you are gracious.
I have abused your grace;
    you are patient.
I have tried your patience;
    you bear with me in love.
I have tested your love;
    you are faithful.
I am unfaithful;
    you are infinite.

DAVID CLARKSON

5. A Perpetual Refuge

Eternal Lord,
> you are a perpetual refuge and security to your people.
Your providence is not confined to one generation;
>> it is not one age only
>>> that tastes your bounty and compassion.
Your eye has never yet slept,
>> nor have you suffered the little ship of your church
>>> to be swallowed up,
>>>> though it has been tossed upon the waves.
You have always been a haven to preserve us
>> and a house to secure us.
You have always had compassion to pity us
>> and power to protect us.
You have had a face to shine
>> when the world has had an angry countenance.
In all generations you have been a dwelling-place,
>> to secure your people here,
>>> or entertain them above.
Your providence is not wearied
>> nor your care fainting.
You never lack the will to relieve us,
>>> for you are a refuge;
>> nor ever will you lack power to support us,
>>> for you are a God from everlasting to everlasting.

The church never lacked a pilot to steer her,
    and a rock to shelter her.

You have always been God;
    no time can be assigned
    as the beginning of your being.
The gospel is not preached by the command
    of a new and temporary god,
    but at your command,
        the God who was before all ages.
Though it is a revelation that takes place in time,
    yet the purpose and resolve of it was from eternity.

We praise you, eternal Father,
    for your eternity is the foundation
        of the stability
            of your covenant with your people—
                the great comfort of a Christian.

STEPHEN CHARNOCK

PRAYERS OF WONDER
FOR THE SON

6. O Boundless Love

Jesus Christ,
    what is there in heaven and earth
    that your love has not made ours?
    There is nothing left but yourself.
And what would all these things profit us without you?
Without you, earth would be hell
    and heaven would not be heaven.
For you are the hope of earth
    and the glory of heaven.
This is the height of your love:
    you have given us yourself,
    and all with yourself.
You are our husband,
    and heaven and earth is our inheritance.
Your person is ours, for you have married us.
Your offices are ours:
    you are our King, our Priest, our Prophet.
Your sufferings, your merits,
    your resurrection, ascension, and intercession—
all, all is ours
    that you have, or do, or suffer.

Your love withheld nothing from us:
    not your life—you gave your life as a ransom for us;
    not your blood—you washed us in your blood.

O boundless love!
Oh, the unsearchable riches of your love!
O happy souls that have interest in this love,
in these riches!

How may we despise the pride of those
who count themselves great and rich in the world!
Their large domains and greatest possessions
are but as a point compared with ours,
whose poverty they despise.
We have riches that they know not of.
We have more than they can desire,
even if their desires be as wide as hell.
We have more than they can imagine,
even if their thoughts stretch
as wide as angelic apprehension.
There is no valuing of our revenues,
no measuring of our possessions,
no bounds of our inheritance;
it is infinite.
God, and heaven, and earth is our portion.

Your love has done this for us, and we praise you.
You have given all these blessings to us, and we love you.

David Clarkson

7. What Manner of Love

Oh, what manner of love is this,
which makes you willing to bear with sin,
 and to continue to be so tenderly affectionate
 towards those who have so frequently committed it!
What king ever loved
 an enemy to his crown?
What man ever was a friend
 to the one who sought his life?
No love, but your love,
 a love with no bounds and no parallel.

Your love made you willing to suffer *with* us.
You remember those who are afflicted
 as though you also were afflicted in the body.
You think yourself hungry, when we want food;
 a stranger, when we are banished;
  restrained, when we are in prison;
   unwell, when we are sick;
    persecuted, when we are persecuted.

Your love made you willing to suffer *for* us.
You who with one word
  caused the vast fabric of heaven and earth
  to start out of nothing,
  who had heaven for your throne
   and earth for your footstool,

were, in love for us, content to become a servant,
　　with no cradle when you were born,
　　　　　no place to lay your head while you lived,
　　　　　　no monument when you died.
You whose splendour dazzled the seraphim
were, in love for us, willing to be despised and rejected.
You in whose presence was fullness of joy,
　　and from whose smile spring rivers of pleasure,
were, in love for us, willing to become a man of sorrows.
You whose beauty was the splendour of heaven,
　　the brightness of your Father's glory,
were, in love for us, by your suffering so disfigured
　　that you had no beauty to attract us.
You in whose sight the heavens are not clean,
were, in love for us, content to bear our sins,
　　to be wounded for our transgressions,
　　　　to be made a curse,
　　　　　　to be sold as a slave,
　　　　　　　　to die a base and cruel death.
You who were your Father's love and delight,
　　rejoicing before him from eternity,
　　and in whom alone his soul was well pleased,
bore, out of love for us,
　　the inconceivable burden of your Father's wrath,
　　which would have sunk the whole world into hell.
Is it not enough, dearest Saviour,
　　　　for you to condescend to pray and weep for us?

Will you also bleed and die for us?
Is it not enough to feel the cruelty of humanity?
Will you also undergo the wrath of God?

Oh, what transcendent love!
What tongue can express it?
What heart can conceive it?
Heaven and earth are astonished at it.
The thoughts of men and angels are far below it.
Oh, the height, depth, breadth and length of your love!
Our thoughts are swallowed up in its depths,
and there they must lie until glory elevates them,
when we shall have no other employment
but to praise, and admire, and adore your love.

DAVID CLARKSON

8. I Will Bear All

Lord Jesus Christ, we worship and adore you.
As God, you are in the bosom of your Father;
    as man, you are in the womb of your mother.
As God, you fill all things;
    as man, you are confined to a cradle.
As God, you are clothed in a robe of glory;
    as man, you are wrapped in coarse swaddling bands.
As God, you are encircled by millions of bright angels;
    as man, you are in the company of Joseph and Mary.
As God, you are all-sufficient and without need;
    as man, you submit to an inglorious condition.
With what less than ravishment of spirit can I behold you,
who from everlasting were clothed with glory,
    now wrapped in rags, cradled in a manger,
    exposed to hunger, weariness, danger, contempt?
Into what ecstasies may I be cast,
to see the Judge of all the world accused,
to see the Lord of life dying on the tree of shame,
to see the eternal Son struggling with his Father's wrath?
Oh, where has your love to mankind carried you?
Had you sent creatures to serve us,
    prophets to advise us, angels to minister to us;
    had you come to visit us, to weep for us,
    that would have been a great mercy.

But you came yourself, and you came
    to lay down your lifeblood, all for your people.
That you should be cursed, that we might be blessed;
    forsaken, that we might not be forsaken;
    condemned, that we might be acquitted:
oh, what raptures of spirit can be sufficient
    for the admiration of this so infinite mercy?

Be swallowed up, O my soul, in this depth of divine love.
Listen to the attributes of God.
    Mercy cries, "I am abused."
      Patience cries, "I am despised."
        Goodness cries, "I am wronged."
          Holiness cries, "I am contradicted."
    All come to the Father crying out for justice.
Listen as Christ steps in: "I will bear all, and satisfy all."
Look upon him as he hangs on the cross,
all naked, all torn, all bloody, between heaven and earth,
as if cast out of heaven and thrown up by earth.
    O love more deep than hell!
    O love more high than heaven!
      The brightest seraphim are but as sparkles
      to the mighty flame of love in the heart of Jesus.

ISAAC AMBROSE

9. A MASS OF LOVE

Lord Jesus Christ,
what comforts you give to poor, broken-hearted believers!
If heaven and earth were compressed
    into one mass of pure gold,
    it would not weigh the thousandth part
    of your love to a soul—even to me, a poor prisoner.
You are the fairest Rose in all God's paradise,
    infinitely above all imaginable and created glory.
For your fire is hotter than any other fire;
    your love sweeter than common love;
      your beauty surpasses all other beauty.
Oh, that others would fall in love with you!
Yet all of us together could not love you enough,
who are the Son of the Father's love, and God's delight.

Lord, grant that the meeting of your people
may be a trysting-place
    where we may feast together,
    and drink that pure river of the water of life,
    that flows from the throne of God and of the Lamb.

SAMUEL RUTHERFORD

10. THE SUN AND THE CENTRE

There is an excellence in knowing you, Lord Jesus,
    above all other knowledge in the world.
There is nothing more pleasing and comfortable,
    more animating and enlivening.
You are the sun and centre of all divine truth.
Only you are the whole of our happiness:
the sun to enlighten us,
    the physician to heal us,
        the wall of fire to defend us,
            the friend to comfort us,
                the pearl to enrich us,
                    the ark to support us.
You are the rock to sustain us
    under the heaviest pressures;
    as a hiding place from the wind,
        as a covert from the tempest,
            as rivers of water in a dry place,
                and as the shadow in a weary land.
Only you are the ladder between earth and heaven,
    the Mediator between God and man.

All other things are vanities,
    but you are real, solid, substantial, excellent, glorious.

All other things are temporary,
  but you are an enduring substance.
All other things are thorns and vex our spirits,
  but you are full of joy and comfort, altogether lovely.

What, must I turn away from my sins?
  Why, there before me are the graces of your Spirit.
Must I turn away from corrupting company?
  There before me is fellowship
    with you and your Father.
Must I turn away from honours and glory?
  There before me is the privilege of adoption.
Must I turn away from worldly riches?
  There before me are the riches of your grace.
Must I turn away from sinful pleasures?
  There before me is fullness of joy.
Must I turn away from my own righteousness?
  There before me is your perfect righteousness.
Oh, who would fill their coffers with pebbles,
  when they may have gold and silver?
Lord Jesus, you turned away from heaven for me;
  how much more should I turn away
  from earthly things!
Oh, may your melting love win my heart to you,
  and wean me off all other things!

ISAAC AMBROSE

PRAYERS OF DEPENDENCE ON THE SPIRIT

11. The Wisdom of Heaven

Spirit of God, you are the Wisdom of heaven,
    never leading us into folly.
Spirit of God, you are a Spirit of Love,
    delighting always to do good.
Spirit of God, you are a Spirit of Concord,
    ever for the unity of believers; abhorring division.
Spirit of God, you are a Spirit of Humility and Self-Denial,
    making us little in our own eyes; abhorring pride.
Spirit of God, you are a Spirit of Meekness,
    for patience and forbearance; abhorring envy.
Spirit of God, you are a Spirit of Zeal for God,
    resolving us against known sin; abhorring indifference.
Spirit of God, you are a Spirit of Mortification,
    contending against the flesh; abhorring selfish licence.

Enable us, we pray, to discern your influence in our lives:
    never contradicting the doctrine of Christ,
    always moving us towards conformity to him;
    never ludicrous, impertinent, or hurtful,
    always tending to our good,
    perfecting of our sanctification and obedience,
    never trivial, never distracting, never disturbing,
    never driving us from God or making us unfit for duty,

but always subjecting all to God,
   raising our hearts to him,
      making us spiritual and divine,
        and ever for God's glory.

Spirit of God,
may we never quench your influence in our lives,
   either by wilful sin or by neglecting your help.
You are the spring to all your spiritual motions;
      the wind in our sails.
We can do nothing without you.
Therefore we pray for your help.
And when you knock at the door,
   may we not behave as if we have not heard you:
   but may we obey speedily, thoroughly, constantly.

May we not neglect the means you have appointed:
   let us be constant in prayer, meditation,
      hearing, reading,
        expecting your blessing.
Like a farmer who ploughs and sows,
   expecting the sun and rain to yield a harvest,
may we sow according to your appointed means,
   and may you grant in us a harvest of life and holiness.

RICHARD BAXTER

12. PURIFY AND CLEANSE US

Lord God, we come to you aware of
    the darkness and ignorance of our minds,
        the perversity and stubbornness of our wills,
            the disorder and irregularity of our affections.
Cure our evil frame through the work of your Holy Spirit.
May he rectify and renovate our nature,
    giving us a new understanding,
        a new heart,
            new affections,
renewing our whole soul into your image.

We thank you for his work of regeneration
    that need not be repeated:
    our nature has been cleansed
    and your image has been restored.
May we now be cleansed from our sins,
    as is so frequently promised we shall be,
    as is so frequently prescribed we should be,
    without which we cannot have true holiness in us.

Help us to labour after, and endeavour to grow in,
    this renovation of our nature by your Holy Spirit.
Grant us, we pray,
    more saving light in our minds,
    more heavenly love in our wills and affections,

more constant readiness to obedience in our hearts,
    that we might be more pure,
    and more cleansed from the pollution of sin.

May your Holy Spirit purify and cleanse us
    by strengthening our souls
    for all holy duties
        and against all actual sins.
Having given us a principle of purity and holiness,
    may your Spirit act in our duties of obedience
    and in opposition to sin.

But if we sin and are defiled, how shall we be cleansed?
    You are faithful and just and will forgive us our sins
    and purify us from all unrighteousness.
The blood of Jesus Christ your Son
    cleanses us from all sin.
And so we pray,
    may the blood of Christ,
    purge us from our sins,
    by a special application of it to our souls
              by your Holy Spirit.

JOHN OWEN

13. My Comforter

Holy Spirit, I thank you
    for your own great love and infinite condescension.
You willingly come forth from the Father
        to be my comforter.
You knew what I was, and what I could do,
    that I would grieve you, provoke you, quench you,
           and defile your dwelling-place.
And yet you came to be my comforter.

And now you pursue my progress in sanctification,
    and all the fruits of regeneration,
    dissuading me from evil.
In return, may I pursue holiness
    on the account of your love, kindness and tenderness.
May I delight you with my obedience
    and not grieve you with evils and follies.

Holy Spirit, in your infinite love and kindness towards me,
    you have condescended to be my comforter;
    and you do so willingly, freely, powerfully.
I have received so much from you!
In the multitude of my perplexities
    how you have refreshed my soul!
Can I live one day without your consolations?

And then shall I grieve you
    by my negligence, sin, and folly?
No, may your love constrain me:
    may every step I take be well-pleasing to you.

May I have communion with you,
as I consider you by faith to be the source
    of all the supplies and assistance I have by grace;
    of all the good intentions and motives in my heart;
    of all my strivings and contendings against sin.
They come from your love, kindness and tenderness,
and so may I be careful and watchful to employ them.

As you shed abroad the love of God in my heart,
    as you witness to my adoption,
        as I consider your presence,
            and ponder your love, goodness and kindness,
so may I be filled with reverence for you
    and labour to keep your temple pure and holy.
I return praise, thanks, honour, glory and blessing to you
    for the many mercies and privileges
                which I receive from you.

John Owen

14. GIVE US WINGS

Holy Spirit, our hearts are naturally polluted:
    come into them, we pray,
        and work sin out,
            and work grace in.
Make our hearts temples of purity
    and a paradise for pleasantness.
Sanctify our imaginations,
    causing them to mint holy meditations.
Sanctify our wills,
    biasing them to good,
    so it will be as delightful for us to serve God
    as once it was to sin against him.
Perfume us with holiness
    and make our hearts a map of heaven.

Holy Spirit, we praise you for your life-giving power.
Our hearts are listless towards our duty:
come and lift them up.
    Make our love ardent, and our hope lively.
    Remove the weights of the soul and give it wings.

Holy Spirit, we praise you for your ruling power.
You sit paramount in the soul:
    exercise authority over our hearts,
    bringing every thought to the obedience of Christ.

Holy Spirit, we praise you for your calming power.
You turn flint into flesh:
   soften our hard hearts
   so they yield to divine impressions.

Holy Spirit, we praise you for your comforting power.
You cheer us and revive us:
   be our Comforter.

Show us that we are in a state of grace.
When we cannot see our riches,
   spell out our adoption,
   give us a ravishing sight of God's love,
   carry us to the blood of Christ,
   enable us to drink the waters of justification
      which run out of Christ's side,
   apply what Christ has purchased.
   Show us that our sins are done away in Christ,
      and though we ourselves are stained and spotted,
      we are undefiled in our Head.

THOMAS WATSON

15. ALL GLORIOUS WITHIN

O Lord, give me yourself,
    for that gift contains all gifts.
Oh, give me your Spirit,
and you cannot but with him
    give me all things.
Oh, what longings!
Oh, what pantings and gaspings
    should there be in my spirit
    after this Spirit!

Come, Holy Spirit.
Oh, come and dwell in my soul!
I know you will make the place
    where you dwell glorious.
If I have your presence,
    then I shall be all glorious within.

ISAAC AMBROSE

PRAYERS OF GRATITUDE

16. Filled with Good

By night when others soundly slept,
And had at once both ease and rest,
My waking eyes were open kept
And so to lie I found it best.

I sought Him whom my soul did love,
With tears I sought Him earnestly;
He bowed His ear down from above.
In vain I did not seek or cry.

My hungry soul He filled with good,
He in His bottle put my tears,
My smarting wounds washed in His blood,
And banished thence my doubts and fears.

What to my Saviour shall I give,
Who freely hath done this for me?
I'll serve Him here whilst I shall live
And love Him to eternity.

Anne Bradstreet

17. A Thousand Pleasures

Oh, in what language shall my flame break forth?
What can I say but this, that my heart admires you,
    and adores you, and loves you?
My little vessel is as full as it can hold;
    and I would pour out all that fullness before you,
    that it may grow capable of receiving more and more.
You are my hope and my help.
When I set myself to converse with you,
    a thousand delightful thoughts spring up at once;
    a thousand sources of pleasure are unsealed,
    and flow in upon my soul with such refreshment
    that they seem to crowd into a moment
        the happiness of days, and weeks, and months.

I bless you for that body which you have given me,
    and which you preserve in its strength and vigour,
    not only capable of relishing the pleasures you provide,
    but capable also of acting with life in your service.
I praise you for that royal bounty
    with which you provide the daily support of mankind,
    and of my family in particular.
I bless you, too, that I can share it with friends;
    and for family and friends who serve me in my need.
I thank you that, through your favour,

I feel for those in need and can provide them with relief.
For you are the great Author
    of every benevolent inclination,
        of every prudent scheme,
            of every attempt to spread happiness
                        or lessen distress.
I adore you for the streams that water Paradise,
    and make it an ever-growing delight
    for those once dear to me on earth.

I adore you yet more for what you are in yourself:
that infinite perfection which makes you your own end,
    and your own happiness.
O Lord—the first, greatest, fairest of all objects—
    possess my soul!
In every hunger, I hunger for you.
    In every thirst, I thirst for you.
        In every weariness, I long to rest in you.
            In every joy, I rejoice in you.
May I press on towards you, until all my desires
    be fulfilled in the eternal enjoyment of you!

PHILIP DODDRIDGE

18. What Shall I Render?

In my distress I sought the Lord
When naught on earth could comfort give,
And when my soul these things abhorred,
Then, Lord, Thou said'st unto me, "Live."

Thou knowest the sorrows that I felt;
My sobs and groans were heard of Thee,
And how in sweat I seemed to melt
Thou help'st and Thou regardest me.

My wasted flesh Thou didst restore,
My feeble loins didst gird with strength,
Yea, when I was most low and poor,
I said I shall praise Thee at length.

What shall I render to my God
For all His bounty showed to me?
E'en for His mercies in His rod,
Where pity most of all I see.

My heart I wholly give to Thee;
Oh make it fruitful, faithful Lord.
My life shall dedicated be
To praise in thought, in deed, in word.

Thou know'st no life I did require
Longer than still Thy name to praise,
Nor worthy things on earth desire,
In drawing out these wretched days.

Thy name and praise to celebrate,
For ever, Lord, is my request.
Oh, grant I do it in this state,
And then with Thee, which is the best.

ANNE BRADSTREET

19. Fountain of Goodness

Have you taken God for your happiness?
What is the source of your greatest satisfaction?
Go into the gardens of pleasure
    and gather all the fragrant flowers there.
Go to the treasures of mammon
    and carry away as much as you desire.
Go to the towers and trophies of honour
    and receive a name like the great men of earth.
Would any of these, would all of these, satisfy you,
    and make you count yourself happy?

Eternal fountain of goodness,
may I wade into your divine excellencies,
    the store of your mercies,
        the hiding place of your power,
            the unfathomable depths of your all-sufficiency.
May this suit me best and please me most.
    May I say: "It is good to be here;
        here I pitch my tent;
            here will I live and die."
May I let go of the world for your sake,
    for then it will be well between you and me.
Then I will be happy; happy that ever I was born.

If you can make me happy, then I must be happy,
    for I have taken the Lord to be my God.
May I say to Christ what he said to us,
        "Your Father shall be my Father,
            and your God my God."
As by your grace I turn to you,
    cure the fatal misery of the fall;
    turn my heart from its idols to you, the living God.
May my soul say:
    "Lord, where shall I go?
        You have the words of eternal life.'
Here may I centre,
    here may I settle.
May this be the entrance of heaven to me.
May I see my interest in you.

JOSEPH ALLEINE

20. Heaped Up Happiness

Lord God, you are glorious and happy in yourself
and you make glorious and happy
   those who enjoy you as their portion.
All the blessing of the people of God stands in this:
   you are our God,
      you are our portion,
         you are our inheritance.
Oh, the heaped up happiness
   of those whose God is the Lord;
      a happiness so great and so glorious,
      it cannot be conceived, and cannot be uttered!
All the blessing of this world cannot make us happy,
   except we have you to boot.
Nothing can make us truly miserable
   when you are our portion,
and nothing can make someone truly happy
   when you are not their portion.
You are the author of all true happiness;
   the donor of all true happiness;
      the maintainer of all true happiness,
         the centre of all true happiness and blessing.

Lord God, you are a treasure no one can take from us.
No friend, no foe, no devil can ever rob us of you.

You are ours by covenant,
   ours by promise,
      ours by purchase,
         ours by conquest,
            ours by donation,
               ours by marriage,
                  ours by the pledge of the Spirit,
                     ours by the witness of the Spirit.
You are not only our God for the present,
   you are not only our God for the near future:
      you will be our God for ever and ever.
Only a power that can out-match your power
   and a strength above your strength
   could rob or ruin our share in you.
But who is there who is stronger than you?
Is the clay stronger than the potter
   or the stubble than the flame
      or weakness than strength?
No, for your weakness is stronger than any human power.
We may easily be deprived of our earthly treasure.
Many have lost treasures
   by storms at sea,
      by force and violence,
         by fraud and deceit,
            by hideous lying and hellish swearing.

But you are a portion that the fire cannot burn,
  that the floods cannot drown,
    that the thief cannot steal,
      that the enemy cannot commandeer,
        that the soldier cannot plunder.
Someone may take my gold from me,
  but no one can take you from me.
Until weakness can make a breach upon strength,
  impotence upon omnipotence,
    the pitcher upon the potter,
      and the crawling worm upon you,
          the Lord of hosts,
      a saint's portion is safe and secure.
Sickness may take my health and strength,
  death may take my friends and my relations,
    enemies may take my estate and my liberty.
But none can take you, my God, from me.
You are nailed to your people
  by your everlasting love,
    by your everlasting covenant,
      by the blood of your Son.

THOMAS BROOKS

Prayers of Confession

21. I Shall Have Pardon

What a condition have I brought myself to by sin!
    I see, I see, I am lost and undone, for ever undone,
                unless you, Lord, help me.
Oh, what a hell of sin is in this heart of mine,
    which I have flattered myself to be a good heart!
Lord, how universally am I corrupted,
    in all my parts, powers and performances!
My heart is a very sink of sin.
Oh, how my sins stare upon me:
    as many as the sands,
        as mighty as the mountains.
Against the God that made me,
    my sins have fortified my unhappy soul like a garrison.
Unload me of this heavy guilt, this sinking load, I pray,
    or I will be crushed without hope,
        and pressed down into hell.

Which way shall I look?
    God is frowning on me from above;
        hell is gaping for me from beneath;
            conscience is smiting me from within;
                temptations are surrounding me without.
What place can hide me from Omniscience?
What power can secure me from Omnipotence?

Yet as sure as God's oath is true,
    I shall have pardon and mercy yet.
Who am I, Lord, that I should make any claim on you?
Yet since you hold forth the golden sceptre,
    I am bold to come and touch.
To despair would be to disparage your mercy;
    to stand off would be once more to rebel against you.
Therefore I bow my soul before you,
    and with all possible thankfulness accept you as mine,
    and give up myself to you as yours.

Come, Lord Jesus: enter my heart in triumph:
    take me up for your own for ever.
O Spirit of the Most High, Comforter and Sanctifier,
    come in with all your fruits and graces
                and let me be your habitation.
O blessed Trinity, O glorious Unity,
    I deliver myself up to you.
Write your name, O Lord, upon me.
I know my flesh will hang back, but I resolve by grace
    to cling to you and your holy ways, whatever the cost.
I have made my everlasting choice;
    Lord Jesus, confirm the contract.

JOSEPH ALLEINE

22. BURY MY SIN WITH CHRIST

O most mighty and glorious God,
    full of incomprehensible power and majesty,
    whose glory the heaven of heavens cannot contain,
look down from heaven on me, your unworthy servant,
    who here prostrate myself at your throne of grace.
Look upon me, O Father,
    through the merits and mediation of Jesus Christ,
        your beloved Son,
            in whom alone you are well pleased!
For of myself, I am not worthy to stand in your presence,
    or to speak with my unclean lips to such a holy God.
For you know that in sin I was conceived and born,
    and that I have lived ever since in iniquity.
I have broken all your holy commandments
    by sinful desires, unclean thoughts,
        evil words, and wicked works;
omitting many of those duties which you require
and committing many of those vices which you forbid.

*[Here you may confess to God your secret sins
which most burden your conscience, saying:
"O Lord, I do here with grief of heart confess..."]*

For these my sins, O Lord, I stand guilty of your curse.
But with you there is mercy, and full redemption.

In light of your grace, and confident in Christ's merits,
I entreat your divine Majesty
    not to enter into judgment with your servant.
    Wash away all the uncleanness of my sin,
        with the merits of that precious blood
        which Jesus Christ has shed for me.
O Lord, deliver me from my sins,
    and from those judgments which hang over my head;
        separate them as far from your presence
                as the east is from the west!
Bury them in the burial of Christ,
    that they may never have power to rise up against me,
        to shame me in this life
        or to condemn me in the world which is to come.

I beseech you, O Lord, not only to wash away my sins
    with the blood of your immaculate Lamb
but also to purge my heart by your Holy Spirit,
    that I may feel your Spirit more and more
                killing my sin,
    so that this day I may with more freedom serve you,
    the everlasting God, in righteousness and holiness.
May I persevere as your faithful servant to my life's end,
    and be made a partaker of happiness
        in your heavenly kingdom.

LEWIS BAYLY

23. AFTER GROSS SIN

O most holy, holy, holy Lord God,
　　when I reflect on your spotless purity,
　　I justly appear before you with shame and terror,
　　in confusion and consternation of spirit.
In shame I hesitate to come to you,
　　but, O Lord, to whom shall I go but to you?
　　To you, on whom depends my life and my death,
　　to you, who alone can take away the burden of guilt
　　　　which now presses me down to the dust;
　　who alone can restore to my soul
　　　　that rest and peace which I have lost,
　　　　and which I deserve for ever to lose!

Behold me, O Lord God, falling down at your feet!
Behold me pleading guilty in your presence,
　　and surrendering myself to inescapable justice.
I have not one word to offer in my own vindication.
Words can never describe the enormity of my sin.
You, O Lord, and you alone, know to the full
　　how heinous and how aggravated it is.
I cannot conceive the glory of your sacred Majesty,
　　whose authority I have despised,
　　nor the number of mercies against which I have sinned.
I cannot conceive the value of the blood of your dear Son,

which I have ungratefully trampled under my feet;
nor the dignity of your blessed Spirit,
whose influence I have opposed,
and whose work I have laboured to undo.
Oh, the baseness and madness of my conduct—
that I should rend open the wounds of my soul,
of which I would have died had not your hand
applied a remedy which your Son bled to prepare!

O God, how much marvellous is your grace,
which, after all this, invites me to you.
While I am here giving judgment against myself,
you are sending me the words of everlasting life.
Behold, therefore, O Lord,
invited by your word, and encouraged by your grace,
I come.
As great as my transgressions are,
I humbly ask you freely to pardon them.
Display the riches of your grace
and the quality of your Son's blood!
Give me beauty for ashes,
the oil of joy for mourning,
and the garment of praise for the spirit of heaviness!

PHILIP DODDRIDGE

24. TO YOUR THRONE OF GRACE

O Lord our God and heavenly Father,
we confess we are unworthy to appear in your sight.
We daily break your holy laws and commandments,
       although you are our Creator, who made us,
       and our Redeemer, who bought us
         with the blood of your only-begotten Son,
       and our Comforter, who bestows on us holy graces.
If you were to deal with us as our wickedness deserves,
    we could expect shame and confusion in this life
    and, in the world to come, everlasting condemnation.

Yet, O Lord, in the obedience of your commandment,
    and confident in your endless mercy,
we appeal from your throne of justice
    to your throne of grace,
       where mercy reigns to pardon abounding sin.
From the bottom of our hearts we humbly ask you
    to forgive our offences and misdeeds.
By the virtue of the precious blood of Jesus Christ,
    may our sins, original and actual, be cleansed,
       so that they may never have power
       to rise up in judgment against us.

LEWIS BAYLY

25. CONTRACTING WITH GOD

O Lord, I am a lost and fallen creature
   both by nature
      and by innumerable actual transgressions,
      which I confess before you this day.
You have revealed to me
   and impressed on my heart my miserable state,
   and made manifest the remedy you provide by Christ.

And now I, unworthy as I am, declare that I believe
   that Christ Jesus, who was slain at Jerusalem,
   was the Son of God, and the Saviour of the world.
   I believe there is life eternal in him, and in him alone.
I do this day acquiesce to this method of salvation,
   and I entrust my soul to him.
I accept reconciliation with you through him,
   and I contract to take you as my God in him.
I resign myself, and all that I am or have, to you,
   desiring to be divorced from everything hateful to you.
Here I give my hand and take all things as my witnesses
   that I accept your offer of peace,
   and covenant with you this day.

Glory be to you, O Father,
who devised such a salvation,
and gave your Son to accomplish it.

Glory be to Christ Jesus,
who, at so dear a rate, purchased my reconciliation,
and in whom I am no more an enemy or stranger.

Glory to the Holy Spirit,
who alarmed me when I was destroying myself,
who opened my eyes to the remedy provided in Christ,
and persuaded my wicked heart to fall in love with him.

Now, with my soul, heart, head and whole person,
     as best I can, I do acquiesce in my choice this day,
     resolving from now on not to be my own, but yours.
I know your consent to this bargain
     stands recorded in Scripture,
     so that I need no new indication of it.
Having accepted your offer upon your own terms,
     I will from now on wait for what is good,
     and for your salvation in the end.
As you are faithful, pardon what is amiss in my ways,
     and accept me, in my sweet Lord Jesus,
     in whom alone I seek pardon.

WILLIAM GUTHRIE

PRAYERS OF
CONSECRATION

26. I SURRENDER

This day, with all solemnity, I surrender myself to you.
I renounce all former lords that have ruled over me;
and I consecrate to you all that I am and all that I have:
    the faculties of my mind,
        the members of my body,
            my worldly possessions,
                my time,
                    and my influence over others;
all to be used entirely for your glory,
and resolutely employed in obedience to your commands,
    ever holding myself in an attentive posture
    to observe the first intimations of your will,
    and ready to spring forward with zeal and joy
    to the immediate execution of it.
To your direction I resign myself, and all I am and have,
    to be used in such a way
        as you, in your infinite wisdom,
        judge most suited to the purposes of your glory.
To you I leave the management of all events,
    and say without reserve,
        "Not my will, but yours be done."

PHILIP DODDRIDGE

27. OUR HAPPINESS TO OBEY

You, O God, are our Sovereign King, to rule and judge us.
It is our duty and happiness to obey and please you.
May we labour therefore to bring our souls and bodies
    into the most absolute subjection to you,
        and to make it our delight and business
            sincerely and exactly to obey your will.

May our obedience be practical, and not merely notional.
May our obedience be deep-rooted and fixed.
May our obedience be constant and continual.
May our obedience be universal, respecting all your laws.
May our obedience be resolute and powerful,
    victorious against temptation.
May we respect you as our supreme King,
    recognising no authority against you,
        nor any except that which is subordinate to you.
May our obedience be voluntary, pleasant, cheerful.
May it be our delight to obey you to our utmost power.

Though obedience is so difficult for us,
yet it is so reasonable, necessary, and good.
For we, we are unable and unfit to govern ourselves.
We are so blind and ignorant;
    so biased by a corrupted will;
        so turbulent are our passions;

so unable to protect and reward ourselves,
that we should fear nothing in the world more,
than to be given over to our stubborn hearts,
to follow our own devices.

But you have perfect wisdom, to know what is best.
You have perfect goodness, with no evil in your laws.
You are almighty, to protect your subjects.
You are most just, and therefore can do no wrong.
You are infinitely perfect, using no unrighteous means.
You are self-sufficient, with no need to lie or deceive.
You are our end,
      our interest,
        our happiness,
  with no interest other than our good.
You are our dearest Friend and Father,
  and love us better than we love ourselves.
Therefore we have every reason confidently to trust you
  and so cheerfully and gladly obey you
      as one that rules us to bless us.

RICHARD BAXTER

28. Holy Fire

Loving Lord,
may our obedience be free and cheerful.
   Though we serve with weakness,
      may we be willing.
May our cheerfulness show the love in our duty.

May our obedience be devout and fervent,
   our hearts boiling over
      with hot affections in your service.
May our fervency be the fire to our sacrifice.

May our obedience be extensive,
   reaching all your commands,
running through our duties
   like blood through our veins.

May our obedience be sincere,
   not merely to silence conscience or gain applause,
   but to grow more like you, and bring you glory.

May our obedience be constant,
   continuing when we meet affliction,
   like the fire on the altar
      which was always kept alight.

May our obedience be in and through Christ
  in every part of worship.
May we present Christ back to you
  in the arms of our faith.

May we love you with a holy love,
  a holy fire kindled in the affections,
    carrying us out strongly after you as our supreme good.
May your Spirit shine upon our understanding,
revealing the beauty of your wisdom, holiness and mercy
  that these may be the magnet
    drawing out our love for you.
In our love for you
may we desire communion with you;
  may we hate the sin that separates us from you;
    may we grieve those things which grieve you;
      may we labour to render you lovely to others;
        may we be willing to do and suffer for you:
          subscribing to your commands
          and submitting to your will.
You do not need our love, and yet you seek it in love.
  Lord, give me a heart to love you,
    for it is my grief that I do not love you more.

THOMAS WATSON

29. STOOP, STOOP

Humble me, Lord God.
Down, down, for your sake, with my topsail.
Stoop, stoop, for low is the gate to heaven.
Be violent with my corrupt nature,
    that I might be holy
        and lie down under Christ's feet;
    that I might quit will, pleasure,
        worldly love, earthly hope,
    and a heart itching
        after this faded and over-gilded world,
    and be content that Christ trample upon all.

Come in, come in, my soul, to Christ,
and see what I want, and find it in him.
He is the exit of all my burdens.
The tongues of angels, even a world of angels,
    could not portray him in his true colours.
Oh, for a soul as wide as the highest heaven
    to contain his love,
        O world's wonder!
Oh, that my soul might but lie
    within the scent of his love.

Oh, but it is long to that day
    when I shall have a free world of Christ's love!
Oh, what a sight to be in heaven,
    in that fair orchard of the new paradise;
    and to see, and smell, and touch, and kiss
    that fair field-flower,
        that ever-green Tree of life!

Lord, forgive me that I let my love rust,
    or waste it on loathsome objects.
Woe, woe is me, that sin has made so many mad,
    seeking the fool's paradise—
    some desirable thing without and apart from Christ.
Christ, Christ, nothing but Christ,
    can cool our love's burning languor.
O thirsty love, set Christ, the well of life,
    to your head, and drink your fill;
    drink and be drunk with Christ!

SAMUEL RUTHERFORD

30. My Covenant Friend

O most holy God, in your infinite grace,
    you have promised mercy to me in Christ,
    if I will turn to you with all my heart.
Therefore, at the call of your gospel,
    I come to submit to your mercy.
I here, from the bottom of my heart, covenant with you
    not to allow myself to engage in any known sin,
    but to use all the means you have given
    for the death and destruction of my corruptions.
And whereas formerly I have inordinately and idolatrously
    set my affections upon the world,
    I here resign myself to you,
    humbly declaring before your glorious Majesty,
        that this is the firm resolution of my heart.
Because my own righteousness is but as filthy rags,
    I renounce all confidence in myself.
Therefore I sincerely desire your grace and assistance
    that I may enact this, my resolution,
        forsaking all the ways of sin,
            and watching against its temptations,
                lest they draw my heart away from you.

I call upon heaven and earth to record this day
    that I do here solemnly take you,

Father, Son and Spirit,
    to be my portion and my chief good.
And I give myself, body and soul, to be your servant,
    promising and vowing to serve you
    in holiness and righteousness all the days of my life.

Because you have been pleased to give me your holy laws,
    I solemnly take them
        as the rule of my words, thoughts, and actions,
promising that, though my flesh contradict and rebel,
    yet I will endeavour to govern my life by your direction.

Glory be to you, God the Father,
    for such a way of recovery for undone sinners.
Glory be to you, God the Son,
    for you have loved me
        and washed me in your own blood.
Glory be to you, God the Holy Spirit,
    for your power has turned my heart from sin to God.
Oh high and holy Jehovah, the Lord God Omnipotent,
    you have become my covenant Friend,
    and I have become your covenant servant.
The covenant which I have made on earth,
    let it be ratified in heaven.
            Amen, so be it.

JOSEPH ALLEINE

PRAYERS FOR TIMES OF TEMPTATION

31. FULLNESS TO FILL THE SOUL

Lord Jesus, nothing is so suited to my heart as you.
You punctually, exactly, and directly
   meet the needs of my soul,
      satisfy the desires of my soul,
         fulfil the longings of my soul,
            answer the prayers of my soul.
May I crave nothing, nor wish for anything,
   that is not found in you.
For in you there is light to enlighten the soul,
   wisdom to counsel the soul,
      power to support the soul,
         goodness to supply the soul,
            mercy to pardon the soul,
               beauty to delight the soul,
                  glory to ravish the soul,
                     fullness to fill the soul.
Health is not more suitable to the sick,
   nor wealth to the poor,
      nor bread to the hungry,
         nor drink to the thirsty,
            nor clothes to the naked,
               nor balm to the wounded,
                  nor ease to the tormented,
                     nor health to the diseased,

nor a pardon to the condemned,
nor a guide to the blind,
than you are suitable to all our needs,
all my needs.
Earthly portions cannot satisfy our immortal souls,
for the soul is the breath of your Spirit,
the beauty of humanity,
the wonder of angels,
and the envy of devils.
So nothing can suit the soul except you,
nor can anything satisfy the soul without you.
The soul is so high and so noble,
that neither rocks of diamonds
nor mountains of gold
can fill it, or satisfy it, or suit it.
We need a higher good,
a more suited portion,
a more excellent treasure.
And you alone are such a portion.
So make me to seek you
with all my heart.

THOMAS BROOKS

32. HEAVEN IN MY EYES

May heaven be in my eyes
    that sin might have less power upon my heart.
May faith give substance to my hopes
    that I might mortify corruption.
May I set the pleasures that are at your right hand
    against the pleasures of sin.
When Christ calls me to suffer unpleasant austerities,
    may I know heaven makes amends for them all.
When the devil would make me lazy in your service,
    may faith present the brevity of the present difficulty.
May views and foretastes of heaven
    give birth to such a strong persuasion in my heart,
    that all the reasons in the world shall not alter
    or break the force of my spiritual purpose.
When the devil tempts me to filthiness and uncleanness,
    may faith present hopes of being a companion
        of the unspotted and immaculate Lamb.
When I am tempted to neglect duty for worldly advantages,
    may faith respond with the glory of my inheritance,
        the riches of the new Jerusalem,
            the hope of my high calling,
                and the good treasure of the new covenant.

When I am tempted to hunt after worldly honour,
    may faith propose a crown of righteousness.
When I am tempted to murmur under the cross,
    may faith assure me that, though the way be rough,
        the end of the journey will be sweet.

So may your promises be like cordials next the heart,
    to keep the poison from seizing my vital spirits,
    and to preserve my soul in holy generosity and bravery.
For your promises tell of rivers of pleasure
    that stream out of the heart of Jesus Christ,
    and the contentment we shall enjoy with you for ever.

May I look by faith within the veil,
    and lift up my heart to the heavenly joys,
    and remain watchful for my blessed hope.
May heaven be in my heart by faith,
    and may my heart be in heaven by spiritual meditation.
May faith put my head above the clouds
    and in the midst of the world to come.

THOMAS MANTON

33. A STRONG TOWER

Lord, I am hunted with such a temptation
    and dogged with such a lust
    that either you must pardon it, or I am damned;
    either you must mortify it, or I shall be a slave to it.
Take me into the bosom of your love, for Christ's sake;
    castle me in the arms of your everlasting strength.
I have no confidence in myself or any other:
    into your hands I commit my cause, and my very self.
Awaken your almighty power to my defence.
You have sworn by yourself,
    that we who have fled
        to take hold of the hope set before us
            may be greatly encouraged.
This gives me the boldness to expect a kind welcome
    when I come to you for refuge.
You have set up your name and your promises
        as a strong tower.
Confident in Christ's presence in heaven on my behalf
    and confident in his intercession,
I ask you to bring the whole force of your power
    to the battlefield
            for my defence.

WILLIAM GURNALL

34. Sin's True Colours

Lord God,
when the devil presents the bait,
   show us the hook.
When the devil presents the golden cup,
   show the poison hidden inside.
When the devil presents the sweet pleasure of sin,
   show us the misery that will follow.
When the devil presents the profit of yielding to sin,
   show us the wrath that comes from committing it.
When Satan promises the soul honour and profit,
   give us eyes to see the shame and loss he delivers.
Strengthen our resolve
   that we keep at the greatest possible distance from sin,
   and not play with the golden bait held out by Satan.

May we tremble at sin, and keep our distance from it.
Give us eyes to see that sin is a bitter sweet
   whose sweetness quickly vanishes,
   replaced by lasting shame, sorrow, horror and terror.
May we fear to lose
   that divine favour that is better than life,
      that joy that is unspeakable and full of glory,
         that peace that passes understanding,
            those divine influences by which our souls
            are refreshed, raised and gladdened.

Help us to see when Satan paints sin with virtue's colours:
    when pride is called neatness and cleanliness,
    when covetousness is called good stewardship,
    when drunkenness is called good company,
    when a lack of self-control is called liberality,
    and when wild living is called youthful tricks.
Help us to see through the deceits of sin.
Help us to see sin as one day we will see it:
when what once appeared sweet will appear most bitter,
what once appeared beautiful will appear most ugly,
what once appeared delightful will appear most dreadful.

Gracious Father, may we reckon the true price of our sin:
    that it cost the best blood, the noblest blood,
        the life-blood, the heart-blood of our Lord Jesus.
In temptation, impress these truths on our hearts:
that Christ came from your side to sorrow and death;
that God should be manifest in the flesh;
he who was clothed with splendour, wrapped in rags;
he who filled heaven with his glory, cradled in a manger;
the God of the law, subject to the law;
he who is the fullness of all things, hungry and thirsty;
the God of strength, weary;
the Judge of all flesh, condemned;
the God of life, put to death;
the fairest of faces, spat upon;
hands that hold the sceptre of heaven, nailed to the cross;

eyes purer than the sun, put out by death's darkness;
each sense aggravated:

    his feeling with a spear and nails;

    his smell with the stench of death;

    his taste with vinegar and gall;

    his hearing with reproaches;

    his sight with his mother bemoaning him;

    his soul, comfortless and forsaken;

and all this
for those very sins that Satan dresses up in fine colours!

Oh, may these considerations stir up our souls against sin,
    that we might fly from temptation,
        and use all holy means to subdue and destroy it!
May the thoughts of the crucified Christ
    never leave our minds.
May they be our meat and drink,
    our sweetness and comfort,
        our honey and our desire,
            our life, death and resurrection.

Thomas Brooks

35. Divine Protection

Blessed God, it is to your almighty power that I flee.
See me surrounded with difficulties and dangers,
    and stretch out your omnipotent arm to save me.
This day I solemnly put myself under your protection:
    exert your power in my favour,
    and let me make the shadow of your wings my refuge.
Let your grace be sufficient for me,
    and your strength made perfect in my weakness.
Oh, root out those corruptions from my heart
    which in an hour of pressing temptation
    might incline me to view things in a different light,
    and so betray me into the hands of the enemy!
Strengthen my faith, O Lord, and encourage my hope!
Inspire me with heroic resolution
    to oppose everything that lies in my way to heaven;
    and let me set my face like a flint
    against all the assaults of earth and hell.
If sinners entice me, let me not consent;
    if they insult me, let me not regard it;
        if they threaten me, let me not fear it.
Rather may a holy and ardent
    yet prudent and well-governed zeal
        allow me never to be ashamed to plead your cause
        against the most profane deriders of religion!

Keep me, O Lord, now and at all times!
Never let me think, whatever age or station I attain,
 that I am strong enough
 to maintain the combat without you.
Nor let me imagine myself
 so weak that you cannot support me!
Wherever you lead me, there let me follow;
and whatever position you give me, there let me labour:
 there let me maintain the holy war
 against all the enemies of my salvation.

And you, O glorious Redeemer, Captain of my salvation,
 the great Author and Finisher of my faith,
when I am in danger of denying you, as Peter did,
 look upon me with that majesty and tenderness
 which may either secure me from falling
 or may speedily recover me to God and my duty again!
And teach me, even from my failings,
to humble myself more deeply
  for all I have done amiss,
 and to redouble my future diligence and caution.

PHILIP DODDRIDGE

PRAYERS FOR TIMES OF NEED

36. OPEN THE WELL OF LIFE

"Come to me, all you who are weary and burdened,
and I will give you rest." (Matthew 11:28)

Lord, I am weary.
Lord, I am burdened with my sins, which are innumerable.
I am ready to sink, Lord, even into hell,
 unless you in your mercy deliver me.
Lord, you have promised by your own word
 that you will refresh the weary soul.
Lord, make good the promise you have made to me:
 grant me ease and mercy at your hands.
 "Let anyone who is thirsty
 come to me and drink." (John 7:37)

O merciful Lord God,
you are Alpha and Omega, the beginning and the end.
You say "It is done" of things that are yet to come,
 so faithful and true are your promises.
You promise by your own word, out of your own mouth,
 to give to the thirsty the fountain of the water of life.
O Lord, I thirst, I faint, I languish,
 I long for one drop of mercy.
 As the deer pants for the water-brooks,
 so pants my soul after you, O God.
Were I to possess the glory, the wealth, the pleasures

of the whole world, and had I ten thousand lives,
I would lay them down to have this poor trembling soul
   received into the bleeding arms
      of my blessed Redeemer.

O Lord, my spirit melts into tears of blood,
   my heart is shattered into pieces.
Out of the place of dragons and the shadow of death
   I lift up my heavy and sad thoughts to you.
The memory of my pollution is a vomit to my soul;
   my soul is wounded by the thought of hell.
Lord, the fury of your just wrath
   and the scorchings of my own conscience
   have so wasted my heart that my thirst is insatiable.
My desire for Jesus Christ, for his pardon and grace,
   is as greedy as the grave.
Make good your promise to me
   as I lie grovelling in the dust
      and trembling at your feet:
open now that promised well of life,
   for I must drink—or else I die.

ISAAC AMBROSE

37. THE ONLY ROCK

Lord God, you are the only rock
    on which we may rest safe in time of danger;
        the only way to quiet our souls
            and to stay the same in every situation.
Sin unsettles our souls,
    but by your Spirit and your word you give pardon.
May we trust in you for life everlasting.
Then may we trust in you for this life
    for whatever we need.
For the same love that brings everlasting life
        will give us daily bread.
When we are in trouble,
    may we find an answering comfort in you.
When we are sick, be our health.
When we are weak, be our strength.
When we are dead, be our life.
You are a rock to build upon,
    a castle in which we may be safe,
        a shield to defend us in times of danger.
You are our great reward,
    bread to strengthen us,
        a Spirit of all comfort.
There is something in you for every malady,
    and something in your word for every trouble.

So help us to trust in you
    and quiet our souls.
For as heavy bodies rest
when they come to the centre of the earth,
    so our souls find rest when they come to you
    and make you our resting place.

Give us true faith, that our souls might be strengthened
    by your promises and by your nature.
Let us not be the cause of shame
    by living an unsettled and discontented life,
    as if we had no Father in heaven
    and no providence upon earth.
For you are an infinite God
    who has made abundant promises,
    and we have a rich Saviour.

May we comfort ourselves with this:
    though we are now cast down and heavy-hearted,
    yet you will redeem your people
                    from all their iniquities,
    and rescue them from all their troubles.
The church must be delivered, and Babel must fall.

RICHARD SIBBES

38. BLESSING IN BITTERNESS

May I bless you, Lord, and be thankful to you,
    as much under misery as under mercy;
    as much when you appear to frown as when you smile;
as much when you take as when you give.
May I look through all secondary causes
    and see your hand in all that befalls me;
    and sweetly sing: "The Lord gives, and the Lord takes;
                      blessed be the name of the Lord."
Humble my soul that I might say:
    "If it is your will that I should be in darkness,
        I will bless you;
    and if it is your will that I should be again in light,
        I will bless you.
    If you comfort me, I will bless you;
        and if you afflict me, I will bless you.
    If you make me poor, I will bless you;
        and if you make me rich, I will bless you."
Humble my soul, I pray, and make it quick-sighted
    to see the sugar at the bottom of the bitterest cup.
May I receive afflictions as your plough,
    your pruning knife, your soap.
Lord, I bless you, and kiss the rod.

THOMAS BROOKS

39. MAY AFFLICTIONS TEACH ME

Kind Father,
may my afflictions teach me to estimate,
    if only with an imperfect guess,
      the sufferings of your Son, Jesus Christ.
Is the wrath of man so piercing?
    What then was the wrath of God,
    which scorched his righteous soul,
    and forced his blood through his flesh in Gethsemane?
Are the buffetings of humanity so grievous?
    What then were the buffetings of Satan,
    when all the serpent's brood lay biting at Christ's heels?
Is a burning fever so hot?
    How then did the flames of hell
    scald my Saviour's spirit?
Is it a heart-piercing affliction to be deserted by friends?
    What was it then for the Son of your love
    to be deserted by his Father?
Is a chain so heavy,
    a prison so loathsome,
      and a death so dreadful?

What was it for him who made heaven and earth
to be bound with a chain,
hurried from one unrighteous judge to another,

cast into prison, abused, condemned, and executed?
What was it for him to endure
   the contradiction of sinners,
      the rage of the devil,
         and the wrath of God?

Lord God, I bless you:
   my prison is not my hell;
   my burnings are not unquenchable flames;
   my cup is not filled with wrath.
I bless you for Jesus Christ,
by whom I am delivered from the wrath to come!

May our afflictions make heaven appear as heaven indeed!
   To the weary, may heaven appear as rest.
   To the banished, may heaven appear as home.
   To the scorned, may heaven appear as glory.
   To the captive, may heaven appear as liberty.
   To the hungry, may heaven appear as hidden manna.
   To the thirsty, may heaven appear as a fountain of life.
   To the grieved, may heaven appear as fullness of joy.
May your discipline lessen our esteem of this world,
   so we discover the excellence of heavenly comforts,
   and draw out the desires of our souls to full fruition.

THOMAS CASE

40. All Good Things

You, O God, are all good things
    and every good thing.
You are self-sufficient, alone-sufficient and all-sufficient.
Nothing is wanting in you,
    either for my soul's protection from all evil
    or for its perfection with all good.
When I am ambitious,
    you are a crown of glory and a royal diadem.
When I am covetous,
    you are unsearchable riches,
    yes, durable riches and righteousness.
When I am filled with desire,
    you are rivers of pleasures and fullness of joy.
When I am hungry,
    you are a banquet of aged wine and the best of meats.
When I am weary,
    you are rest,
    a shadow from the heat
        and a shelter from the storm.
When I am weak,
    you are the Lord Jehovah
    in whom is everlasting strength.
When I am in doubt,
    you are marvellous in counsel.

When I am in darkness,
  you are the Sun of righteousness, an eternal light.
When I am sick,
  you are the God of my health.
When I am sorrowful,
  you are the God of all comforts.
When I am in distress,
  your name is a strong tower,
  in which I may run and find safety.
When I am dying,
  you are the fountain and Lord of life.
You are a universal medicine against all sorts of miseries.
Whatever my calamity is,
  you can remove it;
whatever my necessity,
  you can relieve it.
You are silver, gold, honour, delight,
  food, raiment, house, land,
  peace, wisdom, power, beauty,
  father, mother, wife, husband,
  mercy, love, grace, glory,
  and infinitely more than all these.

GEORGE SWINNOCK

PRAYERS FOR TIMES OF ANXIETY

41. RIGHTEOUSNESS

Eternal Father,
this is my comfort: the imputed righteousness of Christ.
This answers all my fears, doubts and objections.
How shall I look up to you?
    In the righteousness of Christ.
How shall I have any communion with you, a holy God?
    In the righteousness of Christ.
How shall I find acceptance with you?
    In the righteousness of Christ.
How shall I die?
    In the righteousness of Christ.
How shall I stand before the judgment seat?
    In the righteousness of Christ.
So help me to remember Christ, and his suffering,
    my mediator and surety, my sure and only way,
    under all temptations, fears, conflicts, and doubts.

Christ, you are my sin, in being made sin for me;
    and you are my curse, being made a curse for me.
Or rather, I am your sin, and you are my righteousness.
    I am your curse, and you are my blessing.
    I am your death, and you are my life.
    I am the wrath of God to you,
        and you are the love of God to me.
    I am your hell, and you are my heaven.

Father, if I think of my sins, and of your wrath;
    if I think of my guilt, and of your justice,
my heart faints and fails, and sinks into despair,
    if I do not also think of Christ,
    and if I do not rest my soul on his righteousness.
This is a precious truth, worth more than a world,
    that all my sins are pardoned,
    not only through mercy, but also by justice.
Satan and my conscience
    may cast many things on my plate:
    the multitude and greatness of my sins.
But one good word will support and comfort me:
Christ has redeemed us from all our iniquities.
The righteousness of Christ is my life, my joy, my comfort,
    my crown, my confidence, my heaven, my all.

And so, enable me, I pray, to fix my eyes
    on the mediatory righteousness of Christ;
    for this is the righteousness
        by which I may safely and comfortably live,
        and by which I may happily and quietly die.

THOMAS BROOKS

42. THIS IS MY NAME

"[The LORD] passed in front of Moses, proclaiming, 'The LORD, the LORD, the compassionate and gracious God, slow to anger, abounding in love and faithfulness, maintaining love to thousands, and forgiving wickedness, rebellion and sin. Yet he does not leave the guilty unpunished.'" (Exodus 34:6-7)

Will you say, "My prayers and duties achieve nothing"?

"Well, be of good comfort," says the Lord, *"for my name is the LORD, Jehovah, the One who creates out of nothing."*

"That's all very well," you reply. "But my prayers are very weak, and my temptations very strong."

"Be of good comfort," says the Lord, *"for though your temptations be ever so strong, yet I am stronger, for my name is Mighty God."*

"Yet I fear that God is not willing to help."

"Be of good comfort," says the Lord, *"for my name is Compassionate. I am able to help, for my name is Mighty; and I am willing to help, for my name is Mercy."*

"But I have nothing to move God to help me."

"Be of good comfort," says the Lord, *"for my name is Gracious; I do not show mercy because you are good, but because I am good.*

Nor do I wait on your merits, but I show mercy out of free love; for my name is Gracious."

"But I have been sinning for such a long time—ten, twenty, thirty years."

"Be of good comfort," says the Lord, *"for my name is Slow-to-anger."*

"But I have sinned abundantly—more sins than I can count."

"Be of good comfort," says the Lord. *"Are your sins abundant? I am abounding in love. Have you broken faith with me? I am abounding in faithfulness."*

"But the Lord is only like this to his special people—people like Abraham and Moses."

"I have not spent all my mercy upon Abraham and Moses," says the Lord, *"for I maintain love for thousands."*

"But I am the greatest sinner in the world. I have committed all kinds of sin, and there is no hope for me."

"Do not be discouraged," says the Lord, *"for I forgive wickedness, rebellion and sin—the sins of nature and the sins of life; the sins of weakness and the sins of presumption; the sins of ignorance and the sins against knowledge: these I forgive, and this is my name for ever."*

"But I doubt this truth because I fear it leads to licence."

"Do not say this," says the Lord, *"for I do not ignore sin. For I have sent my Son that justice might be done. But if there ever be a poor, flagging, fearing, trembling soul, that desires to know my name, then look, here is my name: The LORD, Jehovah, creating out of nothing; the mighty, compassionate and gracious God; abounding in love and faithfulness; maintaining love towards thousands; forgiving wickedness, rebellion and sin—this is my name for ever."*

WILLIAM BRIDGE

43. CHRIST IS ALL

Eternal Father, we praise you for
the completeness and perfection of Christ our Saviour:
"He is ALL." (Colossians 3:11)
He is the Alpha and Omega,
the author and finisher, of all.
In Christ we have enough to supply all our wants:
for the prevention of danger
and the procuring of good.
We are foolish creatures; Christ is wisdom.
We are guilty; he is righteousness.
We are polluted; he is sanctification.
We are lost and undone; but in him is redemption.
We are empty of all good; but he is a full fountain,
from whom flow our present comforts and future hope.

We praise you that Christ is ALL in cleansing our sin,
and such is the fullness of his satisfaction
that he has not only freed us from condemnation
but purchased for us our adoption as children.

We praise you that Christ is ALL
to fill the souls of believers,
bringing heaven down into our souls,
that our souls might ascend to heaven.

We praise you that Christ is ALL to fill his ordinances.
His word and his Supper would be empty pipes
    were Christ not pleased to fill them,
                      who fills all in all,
    so that in the preaching of the word
    it is he who speaks, not only to the ear but to the heart.

We praise you that Christ is ALL
           to fill every condition with comfort.
The best of conditions without him is not truly good
    and the worst with him is not wholly bad.
His presence fills heaven with glory,
    and his presence fills every condition with sweetness.

We praise you that Christ is ALL
    in granting us strength to persevere.
We cannot rest on any strength we have in ourselves,
    but we thank you
      for those supplies of grace and strength
    which we continually derive from Christ by his Spirit.

And so we praise you that Christ is our ALL
    and thus we are complete in him.

WILLIAM WHITAKER

44. Pleading Christ's Offices

Lord God, by faith I plead the offices of Christ.
Christ is my King, anointed and crowned for me,
    coming to his kingdom that he might govern me.
Christ is my Prophet, anointed by the Spirit,
    that he might instruct me.
Christ is my Priest, consecrated for my sake,
    that he might satisfy the guilt of my sin.
Therefore I will be confident:
    as a king, he is able;
        as a prophet, he is wise;
            as a priest, he is willing.
This is my plea before you,
    as strong a plea as is imaginable.

Lord Jesus, it is your office to do this.
I fail in my duties
    and I am unfaithful in my trust.
But heaven and earth shall perish
    before you, my glorious Mediator, fail in your offices:
        therefore I believe.

When lusts are strong, and temptations are violent;
when grace is weak, and God's ways seem unpleasant,
be my king.

When I am ignorant, and wanting means of grace,
in danger of being seduced, and perplexed in my mind,
be my prophet.

When I sense God's wrath, and the guilt of my sin,
be my priest,
and assure me of the satisfaction
   you have made for my sin.

When I sense the pollution of sin
corrupting my person and my service,
be my priest,
and assure me of your intercession
   which always prevails.

DAVID CLARKSON

45. CHRIST INTERCEDES

"I am opposed here in this world. People are like wolves. They are heartless. They persecute and revile me, so that I am killed all the day long."

What does the opposition of people matter, as long as Christ intercedes for you in heaven! Remember Christ's heart. It may be he allows people to be merciless on earth, that you may look up, and see how merciful is the one who sits above.

"I am much tempted, and I cannot pray. I cannot unlock the cabinet of God's treasures. Alas, my prayers are dull, and dry, without spirit and life."

If so, be humbled by your weakness. And yet know this, that when you cannot pray, Christ prays for you, and he prays that you may pray. Has not your spirit sometimes been enlarged in prayer? Has not your heart felt warmed? Then conclude: "My intercessor above has sent me this gift."

"But I labour under such corruptions! The devil is busy, exceedingly busy, and he often prevails. How I am overcome with sins!"

It may be so. And yet do not completely despair, for Jesus Christ is at God's right hand, and there he sits until all his enemies are made his footstool—and are not your sins his enemies? Be of good comfort, for Christ will prevail. He prays that you might be kept from evil. And surely he will either keep you from it or keep you in it, that in the end you shall have the victory.

"Oh, but I am suffering. And there is none that notices or takes pity on me. There is no one to comfort me, no one to refresh me. I stand for Christ, but no one stands beside me."

Bleeding Christian, bear up! Is not Christ's intercession a sufficient answer to this case? Would you be pitied for all your weaknesses? Why, know that compassion is natural to Jesus Christ. He is a merciful high priest, and can be nothing else to you but merciful. Christ was in every way like you, sin alone excepted. If you are in need, so was Christ. If you are persecuted, so was Christ. Heaven itself produces no such music as heart-ravishing as is the intercession of Jesus Christ.

ISAAC AMBROSE

PRAYERS FOR TIMES OF SICKNESS

46. SANCTIFY MY SICKNESS

Loving Father, if it be your blessed will,
    remove this sickness from me
    and restore to me my former health,
that I may live longer to set forth your glory
    and be a comfort to my friends who depend upon me.
And then, Lord, you shall see
    how religiously and wisely I shall redeem the time,
    which so far I have so poorly and profanely spent.
That I may be delivered from this pain and sickness,
    direct me, O Lord, I ask, by your divine providence,
        to such a doctor and helper by whom,
        through your blessing upon the means,
        I may recover my former health and welfare again.

And, good Lord, as you have sent me this sickness,
    would you likewise send your Holy Spirit into my heart,
    so this present sickness may be sanctified to me.
May I use it as your school
    to learn to know the greatness of my misery
    and the riches of your mercy;
        that I may be humbled by my misery,
        and comforted by your mercy.
I renounce all confidence in myself,
and I put the whole trust in your all-sufficient merits.

You know, Lord, how full of frailty and imperfections I am,
    that by nature I am angry and perverse
        under every cross and affliction.
O Lord, the giver of all good gifts,
    arm me with patience to endure your blessed will,
    and in your mercy lay no more upon me
    than I shall be able to endure and suffer.
Give me grace to behave myself
    with all patience, love and meekness
    to those who shall come and visit me.
May I thankfully receive, and willingly embrace,
    all good counsels and consolations from them.
And may they likewise see in me
    such a good example of patience,
    and hear from me godly lessons of comfort,
    that will instruct them how to behave
    when you visit them with the affliction of sickness.

And if you are calling me out of this transitory life,
    I resign myself into your hands and holy pleasure.
Your will be done, whether by life or by death.
Only I beg you in your mercy to forgive my sins,
    and grant me true faith and sincere repentance.

Lewis Bayly

47. FOR A DYING CHRISTIAN

O supreme Ruler of the visible and invisible worlds,
Sovereign of life and of death,
blessed be your name.

I pour out my soul to you—my departing soul.
Bow down your gracious ear, O God,
    and let my cry be accepted before you.
The hour is come for you to lead me to another world.
Enable me, I pray, to make the exchange
    in a way becoming to a child of God.

Gracious Father, I would not quit this earth,
    without gratefully acknowledging your goodness.
With my dying breath I bear witness to your faithful care:
    I have lacked no good thing.
I thank you for the help I have received from others,
    and for all the opportunities you gave
    for me to help the bodies and souls of others.
I thank you for the pleasant entertainments
    with which you have furnished my table.

I bless you that I heard the name of Jesus your Son.
I bless you for his instructions and his example,
for his blood and his righteousness,

and for your blessed Spirit whom you gave me
    to turn my sinful heart unto yourself
    and to bring me into the bonds of your covenant.
I thank you for faithful ministers and gospel ordinances;
    for communion at the table of my Lord;
    for the refreshments which they gave me.
I thank you for the rich promises of your word,
    which now warm at my heart in this chilling hour.

O God, now I stand on the border of worlds,
    viewing things in the light of eternity,
how unworthy I appear to dwell with your angels.
I look back with deep humiliation
    on a poor, unprofitable life,
    in which I have daily deserved to be cast into hell.
But I have this one comfort:
    that I have fled to the cross of Christ.
And I now renew my application to it.
To appear before you in my own righteousness
    is ten thousand times worse than death.
No, Lord, I come to you as a sinner,
    but as a sinner who has believed in your Son.
The infernal lion may attempt to dismay me,
    but I rejoice to be in the hands of the Good Shepherd.
I defy my spiritual enemies
    in a cheerful dependence on his faithful care.

I lift up my eyes and my heart to him,
    who was dead and is alive again.
Blessed Jesus, I die by your hand,
    and I fear no harm from the hand of a Saviour!
I come, Lord, I come,
    with a willing and joyful consent.

For one last time I look on your church.
I have loved it, O Lord,
and I humbly ask you to guard it and purify it.

As for me, bear me, O my heavenly Father,
    on the wings of everlasting love,
    to that peaceful, holy, joyous abode
    which your mercy has prepared for me,
    and which the blood of my Redeemer has purchased!
And whatever this flesh may suffer,
    let my soul be delightfully fixed
    on that glory to which it is rising.

PHILIP DODDRIDGE

48. My Race is Run

Twice ten years old, not fully told
   since nature gave me breath,
my race is run, my thread is spun:
   lo, here is fatal death.

All men must die, and so must I;
   this cannot be revoked.
For Adam's sake, this word God spake
   when he so high provok'd.

Yet live I shall—this life's but small—
   in place of highest bliss,
where I shall have all I can crave;
   no life is like to this.

For what's this life but care and strife
   since first we came from womb?
Our strength doth waste, our time doth haste,
   and then we go to th' tomb.

O bubble blast, how long can'st last?
   that always art a-breaking,
no sooner blown, but dead and gone,
   ev'n as a word that's speaking.

Oh, whilst I live, this grace me give,
    I doing good may be;
then death's arrest I shall count best,
    because it's thy decree.

Bestow much cost; there's nothing lost
    to make salvation sure.
Oh, great's the gain, though got with pain,
    comes by profession pure.

The race is run, the field is won,
    the victory's mine I see;
For ever know, thou envious foe,
    the loss belongs to thee.

ANNE BRADSTREET

49. FOR THOSE WHO ARE SICK

Lord, grant that those who are sick
    may neither despise your chastening
    nor faint when they are rebuked by you;
    that they may seek you,
        to whom belong life and death.
By the sickness of the body
    let the heart be made better.

Have mercy upon them, O Lord, for they are weak.
Lord, heal them, for their bones are vexed
    and their souls also are vexed;
        save them for your mercy's sake.
Lay no more on them than enable them to bear,
    and enable them to bear what you lay upon them.

May you, the eternal God, be their refuge,
    and underneath them be your everlasting arms.
Consider their frame; remember that they are but dust.
Oh, deliver your people in the time of trouble!
Make your face to shine upon them;
    save them for your mercy's sake.

MATTHEW HENRY

50. WHEN VISITING THE SICK

O merciful Father, the Lord and giver of life,
    we are not worthy to ask any blessing from your hands.
Yet in obedience to your commandment,
    and confident of your gracious promise,
    we are bold to be suitors before your divine Majesty,
    on the behalf of this our dear brother/sister.
We would gladly pray the restitution of their health
    and the continuance of their life
        and fellowship among us.
But if you are calling them out of this mortal life,
    we submit our wills to your blessed will.
We humbly ask, for Jesus Christ's sake,
that you would pardon and forgive all their sins.
Cast those sins behind their back,
    remove them far from your presence,
        blot them out of your memory,
            lay them not to their charge,
                wash them away with the blood of Christ,
                    that they may no more be seen.
Deliver our brother/sister from the judgments due for sin,
    that they may never trouble their conscience
    nor rise in judgment against their soul.
Impute to them the righteousness of Jesus Christ
    so they appear righteous in your sight.

Look down from heaven with eyes of grace
    and have compassion on your wounded servant,
    for here is a sick soul in need of a heavenly physician.
O Lord, increase their faith,
    that they may believe that Christ died for them,
    and that his blood cleanses them from all their sins.
Either relieve their pain, or increase their patience.
Lay no more on them than you will enable them to bear.
And when that hour and time shall come
    for you to call them out of this present life,
    give them grace peaceably and joyfully
        to yield up their soul into your merciful hands.
Receive them in your mercy
    and let your blessed angels carry them to your side.
Make their last hour their best hour,
    their last words their best words,
        and their last thoughts their best thoughts.
And when the sight of their eyes is gone,
    let them see Christ in heaven ready to receive them.

Teach us to see in them our own mortality,
    and so be careful to prepare ourselves for our end.
Thus, Lord, we recommend our dear brother/sister
    to your eternal grace and mercy.

Lewis Bayly

Prayers for the Church

51. DEFEND YOUR PEOPLE

Be merciful, O Father, to your whole church,
    wherever they live upon the face of the earth.
Defend them from the rage and tyranny of
    the devil, the world, and antichrist.
Give your gospel a free and joyful passage
    for the conversion of your elect throughout the world.
Bless the churches and kingdoms where we live
    with the continuance of peace, justice
        and true religion.
Direct the ministers and magistrates of this realm
    to govern the people in true religion,
      justice, obedience and tranquillity.
Comfort your people who are sick in body or mind.
And be favourable to all who suffer persecution
    for the testimony of your truth and holy gospel.
Give them a gracious deliverance out of all their troubles
    in whatever way it seems best to your wisdom,
      for the glory of your name,
        for the further enlarging of the truth,
          and for the increase of their own comfort.
      Hasten your coming, blessed Saviour,
        and end these sinful days.

LEWIS BAYLY

52. A PRAYER FOR LEADERS

Lord, cleanse our churches, and repair their walls,
    so they may become gardens of delight
    for Christ to walk in and take pleasure in.
May her ministers be faithful and wise:
    faithful so they do not deceive others;
    wise so they do not deceive themselves.
May their wisdom prevent deceivers imposing on them,
and their faithfulness prevent them imposing on others.
May their wisdom enable them to discern
    wholesome food for the flock
and their faithfulness oblige them to distribute it.

May our leaders be pure
    with spiritual aims and intentions;
serving not their own honour and interest, but yours.

May our leaders show sincerity,
    not appearing outwardly spiritual
        while being inwardly carnal.

May our leaders be diligent,
    like men in harvest,
        like women in labour,
            like soldiers in battle,
                watching while others sleep.

May our leaders lack favouritism,
as those who will appear before an impartial God.
May they take the same care,
    manifest the same love,
        show the same diligence
        to the poorest and weakest souls in their care
        as they do the rich, the great and the honourable.
    For all souls are rated the same in your book of life,
    and our Redeemer paid as much for one as the other.

May their faithfulness fix their eyes on the right end,
and may their wisdom direct them
    to the best means of attaining it.
May they lay a good foundation of knowledge in our souls,
    choosing subjects that will meet our needs,
    shaping the language in which they address us,
    using their own affections to move us,
    being careful of their behaviour.
Send them often to their knees
    to seek your blessing upon their labours,
    knowing that all their success
        entirely depends upon you.

JOHN FLAVEL

53. WHEN CONTROVERSIES ARISE

Lord God,
when controversies occasion division among your people,
may I look first to the interest of the common good
    and to the exercise of charity.
May I not become a passionate contender for any party
    or censure the peaceable.
May I not overreach my understanding
    or try to win esteem for my orthodoxy or zeal.
May I suspect my own unripe evaluation
    and silence my opinions until I am clear and certain.
May I join the moderates and the peacemakers
    rather than the contenders and dividers.
For division leads to the ruin of the church,
    the hindrance of the gospel
        and injury to the interests of true religion.
Keep me, I pray, from being misguided;
    from being carried away by passion or discontent;
        from worldly interests;
        from thinking too highly of my own opinion.
May my zeal be more for faith, charity and unity
        than for my opinions.

RICHARD BAXTER

54. A Sabbath-Day Prayer

O Lord most high, O God eternal,
    whose works are glorious,
        whose thoughts are deep:
    there can be no better thing than to praise your name,
    and declare your love on your holy Sabbath day!

Heavenly Father, for the merits of Jesus Christ your Son,
pardon and forgive all my sins and misdeeds.

[Here you may confess whatever sins
of the last week clog your conscience.]

Make this Sabbath day a day of reconciliation
    between my sinful soul and your divine majesty.
Give me grace to make it
        a day of repentance to you,
    that your goodness may seal it
        as a day of pardon to me.

When I shall, with the rest of the holy assembly,
    appear before your presence in your house,
speak to me through the preaching of your word.
Let not my sins stand as a cloud
    to stop my prayers from ascending to you,
    or to keep back your grace from descending
        by your word into my soul.

May I hear your word with an honest and good heart,
   so I may understand it, and keep it,
   and bring forth fruit with patience,
   for your glory, and my everlasting comfort.
Keep me from drowsiness
      and wandering thoughts.
Sanctify my memory,
   that it may be apt to receive
    and firm to remember.
And through the assistance of your Holy Spirit,
may I put the same lessons I learn into practice
   for my direction in prosperity,
    for my consolation in misery,
     for the amendment of my life
      and for the glory of your name.

May I feel today in my heart
   the beginning of that eternal Sabbath,
    which, in unspeakable joy and glory,
    I shall celebrate with saints and angels
    to your praise and worship for evermore.

Lewis Bayly

55. SAVE YOUR PEOPLE

Save your people, O Lord, and bless your heritage;
    feed them, and lift them up for ever.
Give strength to your people,
    and bless your people with peace;
    surround them with your favour as with a shield.

(Psalm 28:9; 29:11; 5:12)

We pray for all that believe in Christ,
    that they all may be one.
And since there is one body, and one Spirit,
    and one hope of our calling, one Lord, one faith,
    one baptism, and one God and Father of all,
    may all Christians be of one heart, and one way.

(John 17:21; Ephesians 4:4-5; Jeremiah 32:39)

Let the word of the Lord in all places
    have a free course, and let it be glorified.
Lord, let your Spirit be poured out
    upon your churches from on high,
    for then the wilderness shall become a fruitful field,
    and judgment will be founded on righteousness,
    and all the upright in heart shall follow it.

Let what is wanting be set in order.
And let every plant that is not planted by you
      be plucked up.

(2 Thessalonians 3:1; Isaiah 32:15; Psalm 94:15;
Titus 1:5; Matthew 15:13)

We remember in our prayers
those who are in chains for the testimony of Jesus
   as though we are imprisoned with them,
and those who suffer adversity
   as though we ourselves were suffering with them.
Reach down from above
   and deliver them from their enemies,
   and bring them out into a spacious place.
Oh, strengthen the patience and faith
   of your suffering saints,
   that they may hope and quietly wait
   for the salvation of the Lord.

(Hebrews 13:3; Psalm 18:16-19;
Revelation 13:10; Lamentations 3:26)

MATTHEW HENRY

PRAYERS FOR THE LORD'S SUPPER

56. STREAM OF COMFORT

As I prepare to meet you in this holy ordinance,
    may I be impartial in the examination of my soul.
Oh, that my soul might be so searched to the bottom
    that none of my wounds may fester,
    but all may be discovered and cured!
May I look up to Christ alone for assistance,
    knowing that I am not sufficient of myself
    but my sufficiency is of you, O God.
For Christ emptied himself to fill me.
He laid down his reputation
    to raise mine with you, my Father.
He underwent the rage of hell
    to purchase for me a passage to heaven!
May I have an infinite respect for my Saviour's blood,
    the stream in which all my comforts,
    both for this and a better world,
    come swimming to me.

May I see Christ crucified before my eyes
    in the breaking of the bread
    and the pouring out of the wine.
And may I not forget the cause, my corruptions,
    but so think of them
    together with my Saviour's kindness

in dying to make satisfaction for them,
   that the fire of love might expel the fire of sinful desire.

May my soul by faith put on the Lord Jesus Christ
      at this heavenly feast;
   that I may banquet on his blessed body,
   and bathe my soul in his precious blood,
         and be assured that
   though the pain were his, yet the profit is mine;
   though the wounds were his, yet the balm is mine;
   though the thorns were his, yet the crown is mine;
   though the price were his, yet the purchase is mine.
Oh, let him be mine in possession and claim,
and then he will be mine in fruition and comfort.

May I show my thankfulness to you, my God,
and to my dearest Saviour, for these benefits
   by the love of my heart,
      the praises of my lips,
         and an exemplary life.
At the sacrament
   Christ gives to me his body and blood;
may I in return
   give to him my body and soul as a living sacrifice.

GEORGE SWINNOCK

57. CELEBRATING COMMUNION

With humble and heartfelt acknowledgment
    of the greatness of our misery,
    from which neither man nor angel
    was able to deliver us,
    and of our great unworthiness
    of the least of all your mercies,
we give thanks to you, O God, for all your benefits,
and especially for that great benefit of our redemption,
    the love of God the Father,
    the sufferings and merits of the Lord Jesus Christ,
        the Son of God,
    by which we are delivered;
and for all means of grace,
    the word and sacraments;
and for this sacrament in particular,
    by which Christ and all his benefits
        are applied and sealed up to us.

We profess that there is no other name under heaven
by which we can be saved
    but the name of Jesus Christ,
        by whom alone we receive liberty and life,
        have access to the throne of grace,
        are admitted to eat and drink at his own table

and are sealed up by his Spirit
to an assurance of happiness and everlasting life.

We earnestly pray to you,
the Father of all mercies, and God of all consolation,
to ensure his gracious presence
and the effectual working of his Spirit in us;
and so to sanctify these elements,
both of bread and wine,
and to bless your own ordinance,
that we may receive by faith
the body and blood of Jesus Christ, crucified for us,
and so to feed upon him,
that he may be one with us,
and we one with him;
that he may live in us,
and we in him, and to him,
who has loved us,
and given himself for us.

THE WESTMINSTER ASSEMBLY

58. THE GREATEST PLEDGE

As it is your pleasure to eat with me, and dwell in me,
    so I come to your table.
I freely confess the wretchedness of my nature:
    a selfish creature, whose very soul is sold under sin;
    a wretched person, clothed with a body of death.
Yet, Lord, seeing as you call sinners
    and all those with heavy loads,
        I see no reason why I should stay behind.
O Lord, I am sick, and where should I go
    but to you, the physician of my soul?
And though I have many sins and sores,
    yet so abundant is your grace, and so great is your skill,
    that you can with a word
        forgive my sins and heal my sores.
And why should I doubt your good will,
since you were so willing to redeem me,
    though it cost you all your heart-blood;
    and since you now offer so graciously to me
    this assured pledge of my redemption by your blood?
Who am I, O Lord God, and what is my merit,
    that you have bought me with so dear a price?
It is merely your mercy, O Lord.
I am not worthy of the least of all your mercies,
    much less to be a partaker of this holy sacrament,

the greatest pledge of the greatest mercy.
Oh, what an honour is this,
    that my Lord himself should thus come to visit me!
Yet it has pleased you, in the riches of your grace,
    for the strengthening of my weakness,
    to seal your mercy to me
    by your visible signs, as well as by your visible word.
Knock, Lord, by your word and sacraments,
    at the door of my heart;
    enter in, and dwell there for ever.
For I resign the whole possession of my heart
    to your sacred Majesty,
        asking that from now on I may not live
        but that you may live in me,

                        speak in me,
                        walk in me.

So govern me by your Spirit,
    that nothing may be pleasing to me
    but that which is acceptable to you;
and that, finishing my course in the life of grace,
    I may live with you for ever in the kingdom of glory.

LEWIS BAYLY

59. AS YOU TAKE COMMUNION

When the minister bids you take and eat the bread, think that Christ himself comes to you, and gives to your faith his very body and blood, with all the merits of his death and passion. He feeds your soul to eternal life, just as surely as the minister offers the outward signs that feed your body to this temporal life.

When you take the bread from the minister's hand, rouse your soul to see Christ by faith, and apply his merits to heal your miseries. Embrace Christ as sweetly by faith in the sacrament, as Simeon hugged him in his swaddling clothes.

As you eat the bread, imagine you see Christ hanging upon the cross, fully satisfying God's justice for your sins. And strive to partake of the spiritual grace, for Christ gives himself to every soul that spiritually receives him by faith, not by coming down out of heaven to you, but by lifting you up from the earth to him.

When the wine is brought to you, remember that Christ's blood is the seal of the new covenant that God has made to forgive the sins of penitent sinners who believe in the merits of Christ's shed blood.

As you drink the wine, meditate and believe that by the merits of Christ's blood shed on the cross, all your sins are as surely forgiven, just as surely as you have drunk the wine.

As you feel the wine warming your cold stomach, endeavour to feel the Holy Spirit cherishing your soul in the joyful assurance of the forgiveness of all your sins, by the merit of the blood of Christ.

Just as it is impossible to separate the bread and wine digested in the blood and substance of your body, so it is impossible to part Christ from your soul, or your soul from Christ.

Then lift your mind to consider Christ at God's right hand, interceding for you by presenting to his Father the invaluable merits of his death.

Finally, as you have shared one loaf, remember you are part of one mystical body, the church, and therefore you must love every Christian as yourself, as a member of your body.

LEWIS BAYLY

60. REAL FOOD

In the Celebrating of the Lord's Supper

Oh, let this cup of blessing, which we bless,
   be a participation in the blood of Christ.
Let this bread which we break
   be a participation in the body of Christ.
   And enable us to proclaim the Lord's death
                        until he comes.
Let us be joined to the Lord in an everlasting covenant,
   so as to become one spirit with him.
Let us come to share in Christ
   by holding fast to our original conviction
   firmly to the very end.

> *(1 Corinthians 10:16; 11:26; Jeremiah 50:5;*
> *1 Corinthians 6:17; Hebrews 3:14)*

Let Christ's flesh be real food to us,
      and his blood real drink;
   and enable us by faith so to eat his flesh
      and drink his blood,
   that he may dwell in us, and we in him,
      and we may live through him.
Seal to us the forgiveness of sins,
   the gift of the Holy Spirit
      and the promise of eternal life.

Enable us to take this cup of salvation
and to call on the name of the Lord.

(John 6:55-57; Acts 2:38; 1 John 2:25; Psalm 116:13)

After the Celebrating of the Lord's Supper

And now, Lord, enable us to hold fast
to that which we have received,
that no one may take our crown.
And keep it always in our desires and thoughts,
and keep our hearts loyal to you.

Give us grace, as we have received Christ Jesus the Lord,
so to walk in him
that we may conduct ourselves
in a manner worthy of the gospel.
May we carry around in our body the death of Jesus,
so the life of Jesus may also be revealed in our body,
that to us, to live may be Christ.

*(Revelation 3:11; 1 Chronicles 29:18; Colossians 2:6;
Philippians 1:27; 2 Corinthians 4:10; Philippians 1:21)*

MATTHEW HENRY

PRAYERS FOR
GOD'S WORD

61. THE CHURCH'S CHARTER

Your word, O Lord, is a spring of living water,
 a deep mine of costly treasure,
  a table furnished with all sorts of food,
   a garden of pleasant fruits.
It is the church's charter,
 containing all her privileges and her deeds.
It has pious precepts for our reformation
 and precious promises for our consolation.
To the saint who is afflicted,
 may your word hold their head above water
 when the waves break over the soul.
To the saint who is assaulted,
 may your word be their armour of proof
 by which they may defend themselves from their foes.
To the soul that is unholy,
 may your word sanctify them as Christ promised:

> *"You are already clean because of
> the word I have spoken to you." (John 15:3)*

To the soul that is an heir of hell,
 may your word save them:
 for this word alone can make people wise to salvation.

GEORGE SWINNOCK

62. PRECIOUS PROMISES

"If your law had not been my delight, I would have perished in my affliction" (Psalm 119:92). The precious promises of God's word are like cordials to a soul that is ready to faint. They are full of virtue.

Are you under the guilt of sin?

There is a promise: "The Lord, compassionate and gracious" (Exodus 34:6). Here God holds out the golden sceptre to encourage poor trembling sinners to come to him. God is more willing to pardon than to punish. Mercy multiples more in him than sin in us. Mercy is his nature. The bee naturally gives honey; it stings only when provoked. "But," says the guilty sinner, "I cannot deserve mercy." Yet God is gracious. He shows mercy, not because we deserve mercy, but because he delights in mercy. "But what is that to me? Perhaps my name is not in the pardon." The bank account of mercy is not exhausted. God has treasures lying by, and why should you not come for a child's share?

Are you under the defilement of sin?

There is a promise working for good: "I will heal their waywardness" (Hosea 14:4). He has promised to send his Spirit, whose sanctifying power is like water which cleanses vessels and fire which refines metals. The Spirit of God shall cleanse and consecrate your soul, making it share in the divine nature.

Are you in great trouble?

There is a promise working for our good: "I will be with him in trouble" (Psalm 91:15). God does not bring his people into troubles and leave them there. He will stand by them. He will hold their heads and hearts when they are fainting. "He is their stronghold in time of trouble" (Psalm 37:39). "Oh," says the soul, "I shall faint in the day of trial." But God will be the strength of our hearts. He will join his forces with us. Either he will make the burden he has placed upon us lighter, or our faith stronger.

Do you fear outward wants?

There is a promise: "Those who seek the Lord lack no good thing" (Psalm 34:10). If it is good for us, we shall have it. If it is not good for us, then the withholding of it is good. This blessing falls as the honey dew upon the leaf. It sweetens that little we possess. Though a child of God might be reduced to great troubles, yet they will not be forsaken. They are still an heir of heaven, and God loves them.

THOMAS WATSON

63. FILL OUR MINDS WITH CHRIST

Lord God, as we read your word
may we see Christ walking in the sweet shades
          of divine love towards poor sinners,
    and so may our faith revive
        and our comforts be restored.
When our minds are empty of Christ,
    as in temptation and the lack of comfort,
    then they grind against themselves like an empty mill.
So fill our minds with Christ through your word
    that we might be free from temptations and fears.
May the threats of your word lead us to its promises.
And may we, by relying on your promises,
    make them ours, and find their power and strength.
Animate our study of the Scriptures,
    and so pour wine and oil into our bleeding wounds.

And when you have spoken peace and comfort to us,
    when your face has shone upon our souls,
may we comfort others
    with the comfort with which we have been comforted,
    knowing the more we spend, the more we shall have.

WILLIAM BRIDGE

64. BEFORE, DURING AND AFTER

Lord God, as the holy Scriptures have such authority,
    bearing as they do your handwriting and heart,
and as by this star I am guided, like the wise men, to Jesus,
    may I set a high price on every part of them,
        for his sake whose image and inscription they bear.
May my conduct before, during and after your word
    witness that I esteem the law of your lips
        above thousands of pieces of gold and silver!

As I go to read or hear the word,
    may I sanctify my soul, and wash my heart from sin,
    and so with meekness receive your saving word.
I recognise my inability by myself to profit by your word,
        and the speaker's inability to drive it home,
and so I cry mightily to you, my God,
    to open my heart to receive the word with all affection;
        and may the arrows of the preacher
        pierce my dearest corruptions.
May the weight of the word sink deep into my heart,
    that I may receive virtue from Christ
    to dry up the stream of my sin and cleanse my ways.
May the noise of the world
    not hinder me from hearing your voice.

When I come to your word, may I set myself solemnly
   in your presence with fear and awe,
   to give audience to your word as to my Lord.
And, because without application
   the word will be unprofitable,
   may I never draw a curtain over what I see,
     but, disregarding others,
     may I see my own face in the mirror of the law.
My prayer is that the gospel may come to me
   not in word only, but also in power,
   that I might behold the Lord,
   and so be changed into his image, from glory to glory!

After the seed is sown,
may showers of blessings from heaven accompany it,
that from it may spring up the fruits of righteousness,
     to your glory, and the good of my soul.
May the blossoms of my good intentions,
   which sprouted while the minister was preaching,
   ripen into practice.
And may I never rise from this spiritual food
   without giving thanks to the master of the feast.

GEORGE SWINNOCK

65. PRAYER BEFORE THE SERMON

Lord God, confident of your mercy to your whole church,
    and the acceptance of our persons,
    through the merits of our High Priest, the Lord Jesus,
we profess that it is the desire of our souls
    to have fellowship with you
    in the reverend use of your holy ordinances.
And, to that purpose, we pray earnestly
    for your grace and effectual assistance
    to sanctify your holy Sabbath, the Lord's day,
    in all its duties, public and private.
We pray this for ourselves,
              and for all other congregations,
    according to the riches and excellency of the gospel,
    which this day is celebrated and enjoyed.

Lord God, we have been unprofitable hearers
        of your word in times past,
    and now cannot of ourselves receive, as we should,
      the deep things of God, the mysteries of Jesus Christ,
          which require spiritual discernment.
And so we pray that you, O Lord,
      who make teaching profitable,
    would graciously be pleased
    to pour out the Spirit of grace upon the means of grace.

We pray this that we might attain such a measure of
the excellence of the knowledge of Christ Jesus our Lord,
    and, in him, of the things which belong to our peace,
    that we may count all things as dross compared to him;
        and that we, tasting the firstfruits of glory,
      may long for a more full
          and perfect communion with him.

We pray you would in a special way equip your servant
(now called to dispense the bread of life to your family)
    with wisdom, fidelity, zeal, and eloquence,
    that he may divide your word aright to each of us,
    in evidence and demonstration of the Spirit and power.
We pray that you would circumcise our ears and hearts
    to hear, love, and receive with meekness the word.
Make us good soil to receive the good seed of the word,
    and strengthen us against the temptations of Satan,
      the cares of the world,
        the hardness of our own hearts
    and whatever may hinder us from profitable hearing.
We pray that Christ may be so formed in us, and live in us,
that all our thoughts may be brought into captivity to him,
    and our hearts established in every good work for ever.

THE WESTMINSTER ASSEMBLY

Prayers for the Lost

66. FOR THE IMPENITENT

Almighty God,
    with you all things are possible.
To you therefore I humbly apply myself
on behalf of this dear immortal soul,
    this person who is perishing in their sins,
        and hardening themselves
                against that everlasting gospel
      which has been the power of God to the salvation
            of so many thousands and millions.

Oh, that after all their hardness and impenitence,
you would still be pleased,
    by the sovereign power of your effectual grace,
      to awaken and convert them!
You who made the soul
    can cause the sword of conviction to enter it.
Oh, that in your infinite wisdom and love
    you would find a way to intervene,
    and save this sinner from death, from eternal death!
You know, O God, they are a dying creature.
You see a moment marked in the book of your decrees
    which will seal them up in an unchangeable state.
Oh, that you would lay hold on them
    while they are still part of the living!

Oh, let your sacred Spirit work
    while they are still within the sphere of his operations.

Work, O God, by whatever method you choose;
    only have mercy upon them
    so they do not sink
        into the depths of damnation and ruin,
        on the very brink of which they so evidently appear.
Oh, that you would bring them, if that be necessary,
    and seem to you most expedient,
        into any depths of calamity and distress.
Glorify your name, O Lord, and glorify your grace,
    in the method which your infinite wisdom
    shall deem most expedient.
Only grant, I pray you,
    with all humble submission to your will,
        that this sinner may be saved.

To him who has loved us,
    and washed us from our sins in his own blood,
    and has made us kings and priests to God,
        to him be glory and dominion for ever and ever.

PHILIP DODDRIDGE

67. FOR UNBELIEVING CHILDREN

Father of spirits, I pray for my children.
Manifest your grace and goodness
   and wash them in the fountain opened for sin.
As they bear the image of the first Adam,
   cause them to bear the image of the second Adam.
Let your grace be their beauty
   and the eternal weight of glory their portion.
Cause them to hear your voice and live.
Dear Redeemer, you said,
   "Let the little children come to me." (Matthew 19:14)
   I bring them now to you; do not reject them.
   I present them to you
     in the trembling arms of my weak faith.
   Oh, lay your hands on them and bless them.

Blessed Jesus, you know the pollution of their natures,
   the difficulty of their conversions,
     and the boundless wrath to which they are liable.
Let your compassion yearn towards them,
   and your Spirit so accompany their instruction
   that in them you may see the suffering of your soul
        and be satisfied.

And I pray that I may walk in the path of your precepts
   for the sake of those that follow me.

May I be so pious in my words and works,
   so gracious in all my dealings and duties,
   that religion may be written fair through my conduct,
   and my children may with comfort follow my example.
Lord, while others turn off the highway of holiness,
   let me, like the pillar of fire, go before my family
      to the land of promise,
   and shine as a true light
      to direct them in the way to everlasting life.
I pray that as a parent of my children
   I may conduct myself as a child of my God.

Lord, my sons are your sons
   and my daughters are your daughters.
Let your power prosper my labours while they are young,
   so that they may be prepared for that noble work
   which you plan for them in the other world.
And when you send your servants to fetch them home,
   may they be conveyed by holy angels to your side,
   where I and the children whom you have given me
      shall love, and live, and rejoice with you for ever.

GEORGE SWINNOCK

68. FOR OUR WORDS

O Lord, how insufficient I am for this work.
With what shall I pierce the scales of Leviathan,
   or make the heart feel that is as hard as a millstone?
Shall I go and speak to the grave,
   and expect the dead to obey and come forth?
Shall I make an oration to the mountains,
   and think to move them with arguments?
Shall I make the blind to see?
But you, O Lord, can pierce the heart of the sinner.
I can only draw the bow at chance,
   but you direct the arrow between the joints.
Slay the sin, and save the soul of the sinner
   that hears me when I speak of Christ.

Oh, that these people might live in your sight!
Lord, save them, or else they will perish.
Lord, have compassion, and save them.
Send forth your divine power, and the work will be done.
May their minds may be illuminated,
   and their consciences convinced, and awakened.

All-powerful Jehovah,
   who, when you act, no one can hinder;
   who holds the keys of death and hell;

pity the dead souls that lie here entombed,
    and roll away the gravestone.
Say as you said to the dead body of Lazarus,
        "Come forth."
Lighten this darkness, O inaccessible Light,
   and let the day-spring from on high
   visit the dark regions of the dead, to whom I speak.
For you can open the eye
   that death itself has closed.
You that formed the ear
   can restore the hearing.
Say to these ears, "Ephphatha,"
   and they shall be opened.
Enable eyes to see your excellence;
   give a taste that may relish your sweetness,
   a scent that may savour your ointment,
   a feeling that may discern the privilege of your favour,
     along with the burden of your wrath
       and the intolerable weight of unpardoned sin.
Enable your servant to prophesy
   a valley of dry bones
     into a great and living army.

(Isaiah 27:1; John 11:43; Mark 7:34; Ezekiel 37:1-14)

JOSEPH ALLEINE

69. TO MAKE A MARRIAGE

Oh, that I had paper as broad as heaven and earth,
    and ink as much as the sea
        and all the rivers of the earth,
and were able to write the love,
    the worth,
        the excellency,
           the sweetness,
              and the due praises
              of our dearest and fairest Well-beloved!
Oh, then that my hearers could understand it!

What more could I want
    than for my ministry to make a marriage
    between the little bride and the Bridegroom?
Oh, how rich I would be
    if I could obtain of my Lord the salvation of lost souls.
Oh, what a prey would I have got
    to have caught them in Christ's net!
Then my pained breast, my sore back, my aching body,
    in speaking early and late, would all be worthwhile.
Their heaven would be two heavens to me,
    and their salvation would be as two salvations to me.
I would delay my heaven for a hundred years
    if they were sure to find lodging in your house.

Enable me, I pray, to draw up a fair contract of marriage
        between my hearers and Christ;
    to go with offers from the Bridegroom;
        to come, as it were, with bracelets, jewels, rings,
        with love letters from the Bridegroom.
May I be able to tell what a fair dowry they should have,
    and in what a house they should dwell.
Enable me to speak of the Bridegroom's excellence,
    his sweetness,
        his might,
            his power,
    the eternity and glory of his kingdom,
        the exceeding depth of his love,
            who sought his wife through pain,
            through fires, shame, death, and the grave;
            who swam the salt sea for her,
                undergoing the curse of the law.
Loving Father, may they consent to the proposal,
    and say, "Even so, I take him."

SAMUEL RUTHERFORD

70. FOR THE NATIONS

Lord, we pray, as we are taught, for all people,
  believing that this is good and acceptable in your sight,
  for you want all people to be saved
  and to come to the knowledge of the truth,
  and of Jesus Christ, who gave himself a ransom for all.
Oh, look with compassion on the world
  that lies in wickedness,
  and let the prince of this world be cast out,
    who has blinded people's minds.
Oh, let your ways be known upon earth,
  that those who live without you in the world
  may be brought to your service;
  and thus let your saving health be known to all nations.
Let the people praise you, O God;
  yes, let all the people praise you.
Oh, let the nations be glad, and sing for joy,
  for you shall judge the people righteously
    and govern the nations upon earth.
Give your Son the nations for his inheritance
  and the uttermost parts of the earth as his possession.
Let all the kingdoms of this world
  become the kingdoms of the Lord and of his Christ.

(1 Timothy 2:1-6; 1 John 5:19; John 12:31; 2 Corinthians 4:4;
Psalm 67:2-4; 2:8; Revelation 11:15)

Oh, let the gospel be preached to every creature!
And send forth labourers,
   for how shall people believe unless they have heard,
      and how shall they hear unless preachers are sent?
Add to your church daily such as are being saved.
Enlarge the place of its tent,
   lengthen its cords,
      and strengthen its stakes.
Bring your sons from afar
   and your daughters from the ends of the earth.
Let them fly as a cloud
   and as the doves to their homes.
And from the rising of the sun to its setting,
   let your name be great among the nations.
Let the earth be full of the knowledge of the Lord
   as the waters cover the sea.

(Mark 16:15; Matthew 9:38; Romans 10:14-15; Acts 2:47; Isaiah 54:2; Isaiah 43:5-6; 60:7-8; Malachi 1:11; Isaiah 11:9)

Matthew Henry

Prayers for Morning and Evening

71. A MORNING PRAYER

O Lord, we give you our heartfelt thanks
    that you have elected, created, redeemed,
        called, justified us,
    and sanctified us in good measure in this life;
    and given us an assured hope that you will glorify us
      in your heavenly kingdom
        when this mortal life has ended.
We thank you for our life, health, wealth,
    our liberty, prosperity, and peace;
    and especially, O Lord, for the continuance
        of your holy gospel among us.
We praise you for preserving us this past night
    from all the dangers that might have befallen us.
Seeing you have brought us safely through the night,
    we ask you to protect and direct us through the day.
Shield us, O Lord, from the temptations of the devil
    and grant us the protection of your holy angels
      to defend and direct us in all our ways.
To this end we commend ourselves,
    and all those who belong to us,
      into your hands and almighty tuition.
Lord, defend us from all evil,
    prosper us in all graces,
      and fill us with your goodness.

Preserve us this day from falling into any gross sin,
    especially those to which our natures are most prone.
Set a watch over the door of our lips
    so we do not offend your majesty
    with rash or false oaths, or by any lewd or lying speech.
Give us patient minds, pure hearts
    and all other graces of your Spirit
        which you know to be needful for us,
        that we may better be enabled
        to serve you in holiness and righteousness.
Since all human labours without your blessing are in vain,
    bless each one of us in our places and callings.
Direct the work of our hands, and prosper our handiwork,
    for unless you guide us with your grace,
    our endeavours can have no good success.
Provide us the things
    which you, O Father, know we need.
And grant that we may so pass
    through the pilgrimage of this short life
    that our hearts do not settle on transitory things.
May our souls every day be more and more ravished
    with the love of our true home,
            your everlasting kingdom.

Lewis Bayly

72. A SECOND MORNING PRAYER

O Lord, we will sing aloud of your mercy in the morning,
    for you have been our defence.
Because of your mercy, O Lord,
    we are not consumed,
        for your compassions never fail;
        they are new every morning;
            great is your faithfulness.
And if weeping sometimes endures for a night,
    joy comes in the morning.
We lie down and sleep,
    and we wake again,
    because you, O Lord, sustain us.
You have lightened our eyes
    so that we have not slept the sleep of death.
For you, who neither slumber nor sleep, have kept us,
    and so we have been safe.

(Psalm 59:16; Lamentations 3:22-23;
Psalm 30:5; 3:5; 13:3; 121:4)

Let the morning bring us word of your unfailing love,
    for we have put our trust in you.
Show us the way we should go,
    for we lift up our souls to you.
Teach us to do your will,

for you are our God.
May your good Spirit
    lead us on level ground.

And, Lord, keep us from all harm,
    and watch over our lives.
Lord, watch over our coming and going,
    both now and for evermore.
Command your angels
    to guard us in all our ways.
And give us grace to do the work of this day,
    as the duty of the day requires.

(Psalm 143:8-10; 121:7-8; 91:11)

MATTHEW HENRY

73. For the Coming Day

Eternal Lord,
you are the great fountain of being and of happiness.
    As from you my being was derived,
    so from you my happiness directly flows;
    the nearer I am to you
        the more delicious is the stream.
           "For with you is the fountain of life;
            in your light we see light." (Psalm 36:9)

To you may my waking thoughts be directed.
May my first actions be consecrated to you, O God,
    who gives me, as it were, every morning a new life.
Enable my heart to pour out itself before you
    with a filial reverence, freedom, and endearment.
May I read your word with attention and pleasure,
    and may my soul be delivered into its mould.
Animated by the great motives in your word,
    may I renew my dedication to you
    through Jesus Christ your beloved Son.
May I derive from him new supplies of your Spirit,
    whose influences are the life of my soul.

Then, Lord, lead me into the duties and events of the day.
In the calling to which you have called me,
    may I abide with you,

not being slothful, but fervent in spirit,
    as one who serves Christ.
To your glory, O Lord, may my labours be pursued;
   and to your glory may my refreshments be sought.

May I be watchful to observe mercies from you;
   and may gratitude add a savour and relish to all.
And when afflictions come, as in this life they must,
   may I remember that they come from you.
Make me aware, I pray, of my own weakness,
   that my heart may be raised to you
   for present communications of strength.
When I am in the society of others,
   may it be my desire
     to do and receive as much good as possible.
And when I am alone,
   may I enjoy the pleasure of your presence.

May I end each day with a right fear of you, Lord,
   and when I review my conduct, may I be impartial.
May I resign myself to sleep in sweet serenity,
   conscious that I have lived to you in the day,
   and cheerfully persuaded that I am accepted by you
      in Christ Jesus my Lord.

PHILIP DODDRIDGE

74. AN EVENING PRAYER

O Lord, I render to you from the altar of my heart
    all possible thanks for all the blessings and benefits
    you have so graciously and plenteously bestowed;
    especially that you have defended me
        this day now past
        from all perils and dangers
            both of body and soul,
                furnishing me with all necessary good things.

Sanctify to me, I pray, this night's rest and sleep,
    that I may enjoy it
        as your sweet blessing and benefit.
May my weary body be refreshed by sleep
    that I may be the better enabled to walk before you,
    doing all the good works you have appointed for me.

O Lord, who neither slumbers nor sleeps,
    watch over me in your holy providence while I sleep,
        to protect me from all dangers,
    so neither Satan, nor any other wicked enemy,
        may have power to do me any harm or evil.
Give an order to your holy angels
    that they may pitch their tents around me.

Your name is a strong tower to those who trust in it,
    and so I here commend myself to your holy custody.

If it be your will to call for me in my sleep, O Lord,
    for Christ's sake, have mercy on me,
    and receive my soul into your heavenly kingdom.
And if it be your will to add more days to my life, O Lord,
    add more amendment to my days.
    Wean my mind from the love of the worldly vanities,
    and settle my conversation on heavenly things.
Complete in me that good work which you have begun,
    to the glory of your name and the salvation of my soul.

Hasten, O Father, the coming of our Lord Jesus Christ.
Make me ever mindful of my final end
    and of the reckoning that I am then to make to you.
In the meanwhile, make me careful so to follow Christ
    that I may share with Christ
        in the resurrection of the righteous.

These graces, and all other blessings,
    which you, O Father, know to be necessary for me,
    I humbly beg and crave at your hand,
        in the name of Jesus Christ your Son.

LEWIS BAYLY

75. A BEDTIME MEDITATION

1.

As you take off your clothes, remember that the day is coming when you must be stripped bare of all you have in the world, as you are now of your clothes. You have here the use of all things as a steward for a time upon account, as it were. You are to be wise and faithful with this stewardship.

2.

When you see your bed, let it put you in mind of your grave. Your grave is now the bed of Christ: for Christ, by laying his holy body to rest for three days in the grave, has sanctified it. He has, as it were, warmed it for the bodies of his saints to rest and sleep in until the morning of the resurrection. So now, for the faithful, death is but a sweet sleep, and the grave but Christ's bed, where their bodies rest and sleep in peace until the joyful morning of the resurrection day shall dawn upon us.

3.

Let your bedclothes represent the mould of the earth that shall cover you; your sleep, your death; your waking, your resurrection. When you perceive sleep approaching, say, "In peace I will lie down and sleep, for you alone, Lord, make me dwell in safety" (Psalm 4:8).

4.

Open your heart every morning, and shut it again every evening, with the word of God and prayer, as it were with a lock and key. And so, beginning the day with God's worship, continuing it in his fear, and ending it in his favour, you shall be sure to find the blessing of God on all your day's labours and good endeavours. And at night you may assure yourself you shall sleep safely and sweetly in the arms of your heavenly Father's providence.

LEWIS BAYLY

PRAYERS FOR EVERYDAY LIFE

76. FROM MORNING TO NIGHT

Rock of Ages, and everlasting Father,
    teach me so to number my remaining days
    that I may live every day in the fear of the Lord.
Since every day may be my last,
    may it be my best.
May I not undertake my affairs on earth
    before I have despatched my business with heaven.
May nothing cause an eclipse of holiness in my soul;
    but let your word limit me, and your Spirit guide me.
Set a watch over my lips,
    and be the governor of my heart.
My life is a bubble that vanishes with the wind,
    a day that is soon overtaken by a night.
So let me feel how eternity rides upon the back of time,
    that I may prize time highly, redeem it carefully,
        improve it faithfully, that eternity may be my friend.
May I so cast up my accounts each day
    that I am always ready for the great audit-day.

May I end every day with Christ,
    the beginning and first-born from the dead,
        so that I may go to bed as if I were going to my grave,
        knowing that sleep is the shadow of death.
I acknowledge with thankfulness the favours of the day.

Whatever gain I have got in my calling,
   whatever strength I have received from my food,
   whatever comfort I have had from my friends,
   whatever peace, liberty, and protection I have enjoyed,
      you, Lord, have brought it to me.
I receive every day more mercies than there are moments,
   and borrow sums I can never repay.
Lord, I confess there is not a day of my life
when I do not break your laws in thought, word and deed.
As my sins abound, let my sorrow abound,
   and let your grace much more abound.
Though I can never return your favours,
   help me to admire and bless you, their fountain.
     Let the eyes of my soul be open to you in praise
       before the eyes of my body are shut in sleep.
My life is by your providence;
   oh, that it were according to your precepts!
Let every day be so devoted to your praise,
   and every part of it so employed in your service,
   that I may be the more prepared to worship you
   in that place where there is no night, yet always rest,
     where I shall worship and enjoy you
       without distraction—perfectly and perpetually.

GEORGE SWINNOCK

77. ALL I HAVE

O bountiful Father, sovereign Author of all good,
I bless you for the talents with which you have enriched
so undeserving a creature as I acknowledge myself to be.
I confess to what little purpose I have so far put them.
Alas, I have not done what might have been expected
    with the gifts you have bestowed on me:
      my capacities, time, talents, possessions and influence.
Alas, through my own negligence and folly,
    I look back on a barren wilderness,
      where I might have seen a fruitful harvest.
Justly do I deserve to be brought to account;
    but you, Lord, have freely forgiven the debt I owe.
Accept, O Lord, the renewed surrender I now make
    of myself, and of all I have, to your service.
I adore you, God of all grace, that in your grace
    I feel the love of humanity arising in my soul.
May I faithfully distribute all you have lodged with me
    with wisdom, and fidelity, and cheerfulness.
    Guide my hand, oh ever-merciful Father.
Prosper my worldly affairs that I may have more to give,
    and that I might meet many in eternity
    whom you have blessed through me.

PHILIP DODDRIDGE

78. A PRAYER FOR A WORKER

May I serve in my calling with cheerfulness and patience.
Enable me to be subject to my human master
    with fear and trembling in singleness of heart,
    not with eye-service, but as the servant of Christ,
    doing their will from the heart, as to the Lord.
May the reputation of the gospel
    make me holy and circumspect in my conduct,
    lest, by my careless conversation,
    I should give others cause to blaspheme
        that worthy name by which I am called.
Lord, let me so shine with the light of holiness
    that others, seeing my good works, may glorify you,
    and none may have cause through my misconduct
    to speak evil of the way of truth.

May I have an eye to my eternal reward,
    and so be faithful and industrious in my work.
Even if I serve a fickle master,
    in serving my master, I serve you, my Maker,
    and my labour in you shall not be in vain.
May I honour my master
    as one whom you have placed over me.
Though their status be small,
    or their conduct contemptible,
        may I honour them in Jesus my Lord as I should.

Though others mock or condemn them,
let me revere their authority, because of your precept.
Let the will of my master, when not opposed to yours,
be the rule of my work,
that I may obey them under you, and for your sake.
If I am reviled, keep me from reviling in return,
that I may imitate my Saviour.
May I not be lazy in business,
but diligent in every duty that concerns me.

Lord, cause me so to set you before me,
that I may be fervent in spirit about my calling.
May I be faithful to my master's estate and relations,
but especially may I serve their precious soul.
Lord, enable me to serve them faithfully for your sake,
and to serve you truly in serving them,
that I may hear you say:

"Well done, good and faithful servant!
You have been faithful with a few things;
I will put you in charge of many things.
Come and share your master's happiness!"
(Matthew 25:23)

GEORGE SWINNOCK

79. FOR A MARRIED COUPLE

Lord, who are the guide of all relationships,
may our marriage befit those married to the Lord Christ.
Like Abraham and Sarah, may we be famous for faith;
like Isaac and Rebecca, may we live in dearest love;
like Zachariah and Elizabeth, may our walk be blameless.
May the meditation of each other's frailty
    spur us to greater fidelity.
May you be our guide, and Scripture our compass.
How sad to have storms over our heads, and no cover;
    to have qualms in our hearts, and no cordial;
        to have afflictions and sickness in our house,
            and have the God of all comfort far from home.
Whatever stony paths we walk on earth,
    may we enjoy a comforting sunshine from heaven.
And since you have tied this knot between us,
    may we do nothing which might loosen it
        through angry thoughts or quarrelsome deeds.
May our thoughts of each other be sweetened with love;
    may our words to each other be seasoned with love;
        and may our actions towards each other
            be given a relish and savour by love.
Our Redeemer has given this precept, and set the pattern,
    and his name is love, his nature is love,
    his sacraments are seals of love,

his Spirit is the proof of love,
his Scripture is his letter of love,
his providences are written in the characters of love,
his ordinances are love's banqueting-house.
   Oh, then, what love should we have each to other!
May love be the strength
  with which we bear one another's burdens.
May love be the mantle
  with which we cover one another's infirmities.
And may love be the fire
  which consumes opposition between us!
May we cleave close to one another in our affections
  as those who are bound together by God himself.
Let your Spirit so kindle this heavenly flame in our hearts
  that we may be always ascending up to you in love,
    and for your sake be carried out towards each other
      with unfeigned and constant delight.

As those who are equal sharers in gains and losses,
  may we stand and fall together,
    not wasting wealth through our extravagance
    but concerned for the needs of the other.
Let us be more tender of each other's reputation
  than of our own.
And may we imitate your Majesty
  in covering and forgiving one another's infirmities.

May we conspire for each other's welfare,
    and carry domestic burdens on both our shoulders,
    joining together to bear personal hardships.
As fellow-travellers through life,
    may we cheer up one another
        to make our journey more pleasant,
            until we come to rest in the true paradise!

We pray, above all, that with great faithfulness,
    we may serve each other's souls,
    conspiring together to walk in step with the Spirit,
    praying, and fasting and reading together.
Let us take sweet counsel together,
    that our house may be a Bethel, "a House of God".
Enable us, Lord,
    as husband and wife to shine like the sun and moon,
            and our children as stars,
    so gloriously and powerfully with the light of holiness,
        that our house may be your lesser heaven.

GEORGE SWINNOCK

80. MEALTIME PRAYERS

1.

O most gracious God, and loving Father,
    who feeds all living creatures
    which depend on your divine providence,
we ask you to sanctify this food.
May it nourish our bodies in life and health,
    and give us grace to receive it soberly and thankfully,
                      as from your hands;
so that in its strength and through your other blessings,
    we may walk in uprightness of heart before your face,
        this day, and all the days of our lives,
            through Jesus Christ, our Lord and Saviour.

2.

Most gracious God, and merciful Father,
    we ask you to sanctify this food to our use.
Make it full of health for our nourishment,
    and make us full of thanks for your blessings,
        through Christ, our Lord and only Saviour.

3.

O eternal God,
    in whom we live, and move, and have our being,

we ask you to bless to your servants this food,
that in the strength of it we may live,
to set forth your praise and glory,
through Jesus Christ,
our Lord and only Saviour. Amen.

4.

Blessed be your holy name, O Lord,
for these your good benefits
with which you refresh us at this time.
Lord, forgive us all our sins and frailties;
save and defend your whole church;
and grant us health, peace, and truth,
in Christ our only Saviour.

5.

We give you thanks, O heavenly Father,
for feeding our bodies so graciously
with your good creatures for this temporal life.
We ask you likewise to feed our souls
with your holy word for everlasting life.
Defend, O Lord, your universal church,
the government, and the royal family;
and grant us the continuance of your grace and mercy
in Christ our only Saviour.

LEWIS BAYLY

BIOGRAPHIES

JOSEPH ALLEINE (1634-1668) (19, 21, 30, 68)

Alleine was a powerhouse. He was a minister in Taunton in Somerset until he was forced from the Church of England in 1662 during "the Great Ejection", along with many other Puritans. Undaunted, Alleine worked on, preaching daily for several months before being arrested. Even in prison he continued to preach through the bars of his cell. When he finally returned to Taunton his health was broken and he died shortly afterwards. His evangelistic book *An Alarm to the Unconverted or A Sure Guide to Heaven*, which includes a number of model prayers, was the *Christianity Explored* of its day.

ISAAC AMBROSE (1604-1664) (8, 10, 15, 36, 45)

After a period as one of the king's itinerant preachers in Lancashire, tasked with spreading Reformation teaching in a predominantly Catholic area, Ambrose became the vicar of Preston in 1640. Ambrose was a Puritan in a Royalist area, so he had a torrid time during the English Civil Wars. But he survived. Ill health forced him to a quieter post in Garstang, which he left in 1662 during the Great Ejection. His book *Looking Unto Jesus*, which is both rich and warm, is one of my favourites.

RICHARD BAXTER (1615-1691) (11, 27, 53)

Baxter was converted at the age of 15, in part by reading *The Bruised Reed* by Richard Sibbes (see below), which his father had bought from a pedlar along with some ballads. In 1641 he became a minister in Kidderminster, where his practice of regularly visiting everyone in the parish bore much fruit and became an influential model of pastoral ministry. He left Kidderminster during the Great Ejection and was hounded for continuing to preach. His marriage in 1663 to a woman nearly half his age caused something of a stir, but by all accounts it was a godly and fruitful marriage. Baxter devoted much of his time to writing and his output was prolific (including *The Christian Directory*, *The Saints' Everlasting Rest* and *The Reformed Pastor*).

LEWIS BAYLY (C. 1575-1631)
(22, 24, 46, 50, 51, 54, 58, 59, 71, 74, 75, 80)
Bayly served in a number of ministerial posts in England before returning to his homeland of Wales in 1616 to be the Bishop of Bangor. Even as a bishop, Bayly was harassed during the reign of Charles I by the anti-Puritan archbishop, William Laud. His devotional classic, *The Practice of Piety*, contains prayers and meditations for all occasions. In the 17th and 18th centuries it was the most widely read devotional book after John Bunyan's *The Pilgrim's Progress*.

ANNE BRADSTREET (1612-1672) (16, 18, 48)
Bradstreet was born in England but in 1630 emigrated with her husband to New England. Here she began writing poetry. The early years in America were a struggle and many of Anne's poems speak of grief and loss. In 1650 she became

the first American to publish a book of poetry (though she would have thought of herself as British). Her first volume was published without her consent, when her brother-in-law took a collection of her poems to London. Both Anne and her husband Simon were politically active; Simon eventually became Governor of Massachusetts.

WILLIAM BRIDGE (1600-1670) (42, 63)

Bridge was an Anglican minister in Essex and then Norfolk before his Puritan views forced him into exile in Holland, where he became the pastor of an independent church. He returned to England in 1641 and represented independent churches at the Westminster Assembly (see below). He was the pastor of a church in Yarmouth from 1642 until the Great Ejection in 1662. His most famous work is a book on spiritual depression entitled *A Lifting Up for the Downcast*.

THOMAS BROOKS (1608-1680) (20, 31, 34, 38, 41)

Brooks spent a number of years at sea as a chaplain with the parliamentary fleet. After the English Civil Wars, he was a pastor in London until the Great Ejection. He continued to minister informally, staying in London during the Great Plague of 1665 to care for his people. His written works (the most famous of which is *Precious Remedies Against Satan's Devices*) have always been popular for their simplicity and warmth.

JOHN BUNYAN (1628-1688)

In the days of records and CDs, musicians sometimes added

an undocumented "hidden track" at the end of an album. John Bunyan is my hidden contributor. Famous for his book *The Pilgrim's Progress,* Bunyan was an eloquent and winsome preacher despite being a humble tinker with no formal education. He spent over 13 years in prison for his preaching, although formal charges were never brought against him. I'm not sure how he didn't make it into this collection, but Bunyan didn't really approve of written prayers, so perhaps it's just as well. His allegory *The Pilgrim's Progress* would be a great place to start if you want to read more from the Puritans.

THOMAS CASE (1598-1682) (39)

Case started his ministry in Norfolk before moving to Manchester, where his preaching attracted large crowds. In 1641 he moved to London, where he preached at St Martin-in-the-Fields for nearly 20 years. Case opposed the execution of Charles I and in 1651 he was put in prison by Parliament for five months where he wrote his most famous work, *A Treatise of Afflictions*. After his release he ministered at St Giles-in-the-Fields until the Great Ejection.

STEPHEN CHARNOCK (1628-1680) (5)

Charnock was an academic at New College, Oxford. In 1660 he lost his post after the restoration of the monarchy. He spent the next 15 years in London earning his living by practicing medicine, before becoming the pastor of a nonconformist congregation until his death.

DAVID CLARKSON (1622-1686) (4, 6, 7, 44)

Clarkson was born in Yorkshire and educated at Cambridge, where he spent five years as a fellow of Clare Hall. This was followed by ministry in Kent and Surrey. After the Great Ejection he ministered unobtrusively where he could. When the Declaration of Indulgence of 1672 gave some freedoms to nonconformists, he became a pastor in Surrey and then in London alongside John Owen (see below).

PHILIP DODDRIDGE (1702-1751)
(17, 23, 26, 35, 47, 66, 73, 77)

The Puritan era is generally said to end at the close of the 17th century, just before Doddridge's birth. But he was the grandson of a Puritan minister who lost his post during the Great Ejection, and was very much in the Puritan tradition. Doddridge rejected more lucrative and respectable offers to become a nonconformist minister in Northampton. He also led the local "dissenting academy", which trained nonconformist ministers. His best-known work is the influential *The Rise and Progress of Religion in the Soul.*

JOHN FLAVEL (1628-1691) (52)

Flavel conducted most of his ministry in Dartmouth in Devon. He lost his post at the Great Ejection, but continued to serve his people through secret meetings known as "conventicles". Sometimes they met in woods and sometimes Flavel dressed as a woman to evade detection. Later large numbers would crowd into his home to hear him preach. In 1687 nonconformists were given more freedoms, and Flavel's congregation were able to build a large chapel. Four years of blessing followed before his death. His most famous books are *A Fountain of Life*, *Keeping the Heart* and *The Mystery of Providence*.

WILLIAM GURNALL (1616-1679) (33)

Gurnall spent 35 years as the minister of Lavenham in Suffolk. Unlike many other Puritans, Gurnall was willing to submit to the Act of Uniformity in 1662 and so did not lose his post during the Great Ejection. His main book was his three-volume exposition of Ephesians 6:10-20 entitled *The Christian in Complete Armour*.

WILLIAM GUTHRIE (1620-1665) (25)

Guthrie was the heir of a Scottish estate, but assigned it to one of his brothers so he could focus on Christian ministry. In 1644 he became the first pastor of the new parish of Fenwick in East Ayrshire, despite the opposition of the local earl. During his 20-year ministry the church flourished. Guthrie's connections enabled him to retain his post for some years following the restoration of the monarchy, but eventually he was ejected. By the end of his final sermon the congregation were in tears. His book on assurance, *The Christian's Great Interest*, was published in 1657.

MATTHEW HENRY (1662-1714) (49, 55, 60, 70, 72)

Henry was born in north-west Wales less than two months

after his father had been deprived of his ministerial post during the Great Ejection. With little prospect of a pastoral appointment, Henry trained as a lawyer while studying theology in private. Business took him to Chester, where he preached in homes before being ordained as a nonconformist minister. Soon he had a congregation of 250. A chapel was built in 1700 and a gallery added six years later to accommodate the congregation's growing numbers. In 1712 he moved to pastor a congregation in London. He died two years later following a fall from his horse. Henry is best known for his commentary of the whole Bible, but he also wrote *A Method for Prayer* which collates Bible verses to provide a guide to Bible-based prayer on a range of topics.

THOMAS LYE (1621-1684) (3)

During the English Civil Wars, Thomas Case (see above) received more prayer requests for serving soldiers than he could fit into Sunday services. So he started a special early morning service. After the war these "morning exercises" continued in Cripplegate in London, with different preachers offering spiritual council. These addresses were later published in six volumes. Thomas Lye was one of the regular contributors. In the 1650s Lye was a minister in Chard in Somerset where he was born. But in 1658 he moved to All Hallows, Lombard Street in London. Lye lost his post at the Great Ejection, but continued preaching to nonconformist groups as well as becoming known for his children's work.

THOMAS MANTON (1620-1677) (32)

Manton was born in Somerset but spent most of his adult life in London. He opposed the execution of Charles I but retained the confidence of Oliver Cromwell, playing an active role in religious affairs. In 1656 he became lecturer at Westminster Abbey and rector of St Paul's, Covent Garden. Despite supporting the restoration of the monarchy, Manton lost his post during the Great Ejection. He continued preaching in his home and with attendance increasing he was arrested in 1670, spending six months in prison. Manton's writings mainly take the form of published sermons.

JOHN OWEN (1616-1683) (1, 12, 13)

Owen was the brain box of the Puritan movement and one of the greatest English-speaking theologians of all time. For a period Owen was minister at Fordham and then Coggeshall in Essex, but his talents increasingly drew him into national affairs. In 1652 he became vice-chancellor of Oxford University. He was replaced following Cromwell's death and retired to Oxfordshire. He refused various job offers until, after the Great Plague and Fire of 1606, he returned to London to start a small independent congregation. Illness prevented him preaching in his final years, but he continued to write. Owen outlived all his eleven children. *The Glory of Christ* or *Communion with God* are good places to start, or one of his books on sanctification: *The Mortification of Sin, Temptation* or *Spiritual-Mindedness*.

SAMUEL RUTHERFORD (1600-1661) (9, 29, 69)

Rutherford was a brilliant scholar, becoming Professor of Humanity at Edinburgh University at the age of 23. But two years later he was forced to resign following inappropriate behaviour with a young woman whom he subsequently married. It was this, it seems, that led to his conversion. Rutherford started theological studies and in 1627 was appointed as the minister of the rural parish of Anwoth on the Solway Firth. A decade of fruitful ministry followed, but also personal loss, illness and bouts of depression. Rutherford's political activities got him into hot water. In 1636 he was deprived of his post, forbidden to preach and confined to Aberdeen. Among his best-known writings are the many letters he wrote to members of his congregation during this period. When the political tide turned, Rutherford was made Professor of Theology and later University Rector at St Andrews. He served there for 20 years, but his troubles weren't over. In 1661, after the restoration of the monarchy, Rutherford was charged with treason. He died before his case came to trial.

RICHARD SIBBES (1577-1635) (37)

In 1610 Sibbes was appointed as "lecturer" at Holy Trinity Cambridge, a non-ecclesiastical post funded by donations that involved delivering a regular sermon. John Cotton, one of the leading New England Puritans, was converted through his preaching. In 1617 Sibbes became lecturer at Gray's Inn in London. In both Cambridge and London galleries had to be added to accommodate the crowds that Sibbes drew. From 1626 Sibbes combined his lectureship in London with the role of Master of St Catherine's College in Cambridge. Sibbes' writing, like his preaching, is characterised by Christ-centred devotion and pastoral warmth.

GEORGE SWINNOCK (C. 1627-1673)
(40, 56, 61, 64, 67, 76, 78, 79)
Swinnock was a vicar in Hertfordshire and Buckinghamshire until he lost his post at the Great Ejection. He continued preaching in private homes until the Declaration of Indulgence in 1672 allowed him to establish a congregation in his hometown of Maidstone in Kent. His main written work, *The Christian's Man Calling*, applies the gospel to everyday life. Each chapter ends with a summary prayer which Swinnock calls "a good wish".

THOMAS WATSON (C. 1620-1686) (2, 14, 28, 62)
Born in Yorkshire and educated in Cambridge, Watson served as lecturer and rector at St Stephen's, Walbrook in London. Watson opposed the execution of Charles I and narrowly escaped execution for treason following his involvement in a plot to restore the monarchy. When he lost his post during the Great Ejection, he continued preaching in secret. Following the 1672 Declaration of Indulgence he led a nonconformist congregation alongside Stephen Charnock (see above). Watson's many writings are characterised by clarity and punch.

Good starting points are *The Body of Divinity*, *All Things for Good* and *The Godly Man's Picture*.

THE WESTMINSTER ASSEMBLY (1643-1648) (57, 65)

The Westminster Assembly is not a Puritan person, but a whole group of them! The Assembly was called by the English Parliament during the Civil Wars to organise the national church. Most of those attending were English Puritans, but a handful of Scots attended as consultants (including Samuel Rutherford). The Assembly produced the Westminster Confession of Faith, the Larger and Shorter Catechisms, and a Directory for Public Worship. The work of the Assembly was repudiated by the Church of England during the Restoration in 1660. But its declarations were adopted by the Church of Scotland in 1647 and remain defining documents for Presbyterianism. The Confession was adapted by Congregationalists to create their 1658 Savoy Declaration and by Reformed Baptists to create the 1689 Baptist Confession.

WILLIAM WHITAKER (1629-1672) (43)

After a two-year ministry in Hornchurch in Essex, Whitaker succeeded his father in 1654 as the vicar of Bermondsey in London. He lost his post at the Great Ejection, after which he led a private congregation. He has two sermons in the published edition of *Morning Exercises* (see Thomas Lye). He is not to be confused with an early Puritan by the same name (1548-1595) who was master of St John's College, Cambridge.

Sources

Introduction

1. Adapted from *A Practical Exposition of the Lord's Prayer* in *Works*, Vol. 1 (James Nisbet, 1870), p 14.

2. Adapted from Ezekiel Hopkins, *Works*, Vol. 3, ed. Charles W. Quick (Leighton Publication, 1874), p 584.

Prayers

1. John Owen, *Communion with God* in *Works*, Vol. 2 (Banner of Truth, 1966), p 31-36.

2. Thomas Watson, *The Ten Commandments* (Banner of Truth, 1965), p 12-17.

3. Thomas Lye, "Sermon 18: How Are We to Live by Faith on Divine Providence?" in *The Morning Exercises*, Vol. 1 (Thomas Tegg, 1844), p 375-377.

4. David Clarkson, *Living by Faith* in *The Practical Works of David Clarkson*, Vol. 1 (James Nichol, 1864), p 178-182.

5. Stephen Charnock, *A Discourse upon the Eternity of God* in *Works*, Vol. 1 (James Nichol, 1864), p 346, 350, 347.

6. David Clarkson, *The Love of Christ* in *The Practical Works of David Clarkson,* Vol. 2 (James Nichol, 1865), p 11.

7. David Clarkson, *The Love of Christ* in *The Practical Works of David Clarkson*, Vol. 2 (James Nichol, 1865), p 12-14.

8. Isaac Ambrose, *Looking into Jesus* (Sprinkle Publication, 1986), p 221, 398-399.

9. Samuel Rutherford, "Letter #40", *Letters of Samuel Rutherford: A Selection* (Banner of Truth, 1973), p 115-117.

10. Isaac Ambrose, *Looking into Jesus* (Sprinkle Publication, 1986), p 17, 23.

11. Richard Baxter, *A Christian Directory* in *The Practical Works of Richard Baxter*, Vol. 1 (Soli Deo Gloria Publications, 2000), p 71.

12. John Owen, *Pneumatologia* in *Works*, Vol. 3 (Banner of Truth, 1966), p 437-438.

13. John Owen, *Communion with God* in *Works*, Vol. 2 (Banner of Truth, 1966), p 263, 266-267, 271.

14. Thomas Watson, *The Godly Man's Picture* (Banner of Truth, 1992), p 69-72.

15. Isaac Ambrose, *Looking into Jesus* (Sprinkle Publication, 1986), p 397, 426.

16. Anne Bradstreet, "Here Follow Several Occasional Meditations" in *The Works of Anne Bradstreet*, ed. John Harvard Ellis (Abram E. Cutter, 1867), p 11.

17. Philip Doddridge, *The Rise and Progress of Religion in the Soul* (William Collins, 1829), p 517-522.

18. Anne Bradstreet, "From Another Sore Fit" in *The Works of Anne Bradstreet*, ed. John Harvard Ellis (Abram E. Cutter, 1867), p 13-14.

19. Joseph Alleine, *A Sure Guide to Heaven* (or *An Alarm to Unconverted Sinners*) (Charles Spear, 1816), p 59-60.

20. Thomas Brooks, *An Ark for All God's Noahs* in *Works*, Vol. 2 (Banner of Truth, 1980), p 21, 26-27.

21. Joseph Alleine, *A Sure Guide to Heaven* (or *An Alarm to Unconverted Sinners*) (Charles Spear, 1816), p 189-196.

22. Lewis Bayly, *The Practice of Piety* (Soli Deo Gloria Publications, 2019), p 108-111.

23. Philip Doddridge, *The Rise and Progress of Religion in the Soul* (William Collins, 1829), p 466-471.

24. Lewis Bayly, *The Practice of Piety* (Soli Deo Gloria Publications, 2019), p 145-147.

25. William Guthrie, *The Christian's Great Interest* (William Collins, 1828), p 235-238.

26. Philip Doddridge, *The Rise and Progress of Religion in the Soul* (William Collins, 1829), p 377-386.

27. Richard Baxter, *A Christian Directory* in *The Practical Works of Richard Baxter*, Vol. 1 (Soli Deo Gloria Publications, 2000), p 75-76.

28. Thomas Watson, *The Ten Commandments* (Banner of Truth, 1965), p 1-12.

29. Samuel Rutherford, "Letter #17", *Letters of Samuel Rutherford: A Selection* (Banner of Truth, 1973), p 50-51.

30. Joseph Alleine, *A Sure Guide to Heaven* (or *An Alarm to Unconverted Sinners*) (Charles Spear, 1816), p 177-182.

31. Thomas Brooks, *An Ark for All God's Noahs* in *Works*, Vol. 2 (Banner of Truth, 1980), p 27-28.

32. Thomas Manton, *Sermons Upon Hebrews XI* in *Works*, Vol. 13 (James Nisbet, 1873), p 336-337.

33. William Gurnall, *The Christian in Complete Armour* (Thomas Tegg, 1845), p 16.

34. Thomas Brooks, *Precious Remedies Against Satan's Devices* in *Works*, Vol. 1 (Banner of Truth, 1980), p 12-18.

35. Philip Doddridge, *The Rise and Progress of Religion in the Soul* (William Collins, 1829), p 371-373.

36. Isaac Ambrose, *The Doctrine of Regeneration* in *Works of Isaac Ambrose* (Henry Fisher, undated), p 65-66.

37. Richard Sibbes, *Discouragement's Recovery* in *Works*, Vol. 7 (James Nichol, 1844), p 59-61.

38. Thomas Brooks, *The Unsearchable Riches of Christ* in *Works*, Vol. 3 (Banner of Truth, 1980), p 24.

39. Thomas Case, *A Treatise on Afflictions* (W. Smith, 1802), p 62-65.

40. George Swinnock, *The Fading of the Flesh* in *Works*, Vol. 4 (James Nichol, 1848), p 40-41.

41. Thomas Brooks, *The Imputation of Christ's Righteousness* in *Works*, Vol. 5 (Banner of Truth, 1980), p 238-239.

42. William Bridge, *A Lifting Up for the Downcast* (Banner of Truth, 1961), p 270-272.

43. William Whitaker, "Sermon 25: How are We Complete in Christ?" in *The Morning Exercises*, Vol. 1 (Thomas Tegg, 1844), p 501-509.

44. David Clarkson, *Living By Faith* in *The Practical Works of David Clarkson*, Vol. 1 (James Nichol, 1864), p 182-185.

45. Isaac Ambrose, *Looking into Jesus* (Sprinkle Publication, 1986), p 598-600.

46. Lewis Bayly, *The Practice of Piety* (Soli Deo Gloria Publications, 2019), p 266-267.

47. Philip Doddridge, *The Rise and Progress of Religion in the Soul* (William Collins, 1829), p 560-566.

48. Anne Bradstreet, "Upon a Fit of Sickness, 1632" in *The Works of Anne Bradstreet,* ed. John Harvard Ellis (Abram E. Cutter, 1867), p 237-238.

49. Matthew Henry, *A Method for Prayer with Scriptural Expressions* (Ogle, 1803), p 155-156. For a more accessible revised version see Matthew Henry, *A Way to Prayer*, ed. O. Palmer Robertson (Banner of Truth, 2010).

50. Lewis Bayly, *The Practice of Piety* (Soli Deo Gloria Publications, 2019), p 303-305.

51. Lewis Bayly, *The Practice of Piety* (Soli Deo Gloria Publications, 2019), p 111-112.

52. John Flavel, "The Character of an Evangelical Pastor Drawn from Christ" in *Works*, Vol. 6 (Banner of Truth, 1968), p 565-573.

53. Richard Baxter, *A Christian Directory* in *The Practical Works of Richard Baxter*, Vol. 1 (Soli Deo Gloria Publications, 2000), p 50.

54. Lewis Bayly, *The Practice of Piety* (Soli Deo Gloria Publications, 2019), p 193-195.

55. Matthew Henry, *A Method for Prayer with Scriptural Expressions* (Ogle, 1803), p 119-123.

56. George Swinnock, *The Christian Man's Calling* in *Works*, Vol. 1 (James Nichol, 1848), p 218-221.

57. The Westminster Assembly, *The Directory for the Public Worship*

of God in *The Westminster Confession* (Banner of Truth, 2018), p 568-569.

58. Lewis Bayly, *The Practice of Piety* (Soli Deo Gloria Publications, 2019), p 250-252.

59. Lewis Bayly, *The Practice of Piety* (Soli Deo Gloria Publications, 2019), p 252-255.

60. Matthew Henry, *A Method for Prayer with Scriptural Expressions* (Ogle, 1803), p 147-148.

61. George Swinnock, *The Christian Man's Calling* in *Works*, Vol. 1 (James Nichol, 1848), p 141.

62. Thomas Watson, *All Things for Good* (or *A Divine Cordial*) (Banner of Truth, 1986), p 15-17.

63. William Bridge, *A Lifting Up for the Downcast* (Banner of Truth, 1961), p 43-46.

64. George Swinnock, *The Christian Man's Calling* in *Works*, Vol. 1 (James Nichol, 1848), p 170-171.

65. The Westminster Assembly, *The Directory for the Public Worship of God* in *The Westminster Confession* (Banner of Truth, 2018), p 558-559.

66. Philip Doddridge, *The Rise and Progress of Religion in the Soul* (William Collins, 1829), p 314-317.

67. George Swinnock, *The Christian Man's Calling* in *Works*, Vol. 1 (James Nichol, 1848), p 434-437.

68. Joseph Alleine, *A Sure Guide to Heaven* (or *An Alarm to Unconverted Sinners*) (Charles Spear, 1816), p 12, 97, 98, 120.

69. Samuel Rutherford, "Letter #40", *Letters of Samuel Rutherford: A Selection* (Banner of Truth, 1973), p 111-112.

70. Matthew Henry, *A Method for Prayer with Scriptural Expressions* (Ogle, 1803), p 116-118.

71. Lewis Bayly, *The Practice of Piety* (Soli Deo Gloria Publications, 2019), p 147-148.

72. Matthew Henry, *A Method for Prayer with Scriptural Expressions* (Ogle, 1803), p 139-140.

73. Philip Doddridge, *The Rise and Progress of Religion in the Soul* (William Collins, 1829), p 426-429.

74. Lewis Bayly, *The Practice of Piety* (Soli Deo Gloria Publications, 2019), p 138-139.

75. Lewis Bayly, *The Practice of Piety* (Soli Deo Gloria Publications, 2019), p 141-142.

76. George Swinnock, *The Christian Man's Calling* in *Works*, Vol. 2 (James Nichol, 1848), p 510-525.

77. Philip Doddridge, *The Rise and Progress of Religion in the Soul* (William Collins, 1829), p 535-537.

78. George Swinnock, *The Christian Man's Calling* in *Works*, Vol. 2 (James Nichol, 1848), p 42-45.

79. George Swinnock, *The Christian Man's Calling* in *Works*, Vol. 1 (James Nichol, 1848), p 481-487.

80. Lewis Bayly, *The Practice of Piety* (Soli Deo Gloria Publications, 2019), p 152-153.

COMPANY

BIBLICAL | RELEVANT | ACCESSIBLE

At The Good Book Company, we are dedicated to helping Christians and local churches grow. We believe that God's growth process always starts with hearing clearly what he has said to us through his timeless word—the Bible.

Ever since we opened our doors in 1991, we have been striving to produce Bible-based resources that bring glory to God. We have grown to become an international provider of user-friendly resources to the Christian community, with believers of all backgrounds and denominations using our books, Bible studies, devotionals, evangelistic resources, and DVD-based courses.

We want to equip ordinary Christians to live for Christ day by day, and churches to grow in their knowledge of God, their love for one another, and the effectiveness of their outreach.

Call us for a discussion of your needs or visit one of our local websites for more information on the resources and services we provide.

Your friends at The Good Book Company

thegoodbook.com | thegoodbook.co.uk
thegoodbook.com.au | thegoodbook.co.nz
thegoodbook.co.in